Starving the Depression Gremlin

A Cognitive Behavioural Therapy Workbook on Managing Depression for Young People

Kate Collins-Donnelly

Illustrated by Tina Gothard and Kate Collins-Donnelly

Jessica Kingsley *Publishers*
London and Philadelphia

First published in 2019
by Jessica Kingsley Publishers
73 Collier Street
London N1 9BE, UK
and
400 Market Street, Suite 400
Philadelphia, PA 19106, USA

www.jkp.com

Library of Congress Cataloging in Publication Data
A CIP catalog record for this book is available from the Library of Congress

British Library Cataloguing in Publication Data
A CIP catalogue record for this book is available from the British Library

ISBN 978 1 84905 693 9
eISBN 978 1 78450 205 8

Printed and bound in Great Britain

'Another brilliant book from Kate Collins-Donnelly, this time handling the complex and frequently misunderstood subject of depression. Kate provides a remarkable tool for both understanding and managing depression – the Depression Gremlin. This is an invaluable resource for young people who are struggling with the complexities and pressures of modern life, the adults who live and work with them, and indeed for anyone (young or old) who has ever battled with depression. Bibliotherapy at its very best. As a former teacher, a practising educational psychologist who works with youngsters of all ages, and as an individual who has personally experienced the profound impact of depression, I highly recommend.'

– Dr Ruth Slater, Senior Educational Psychologist, Derbyshire County Council

'*Starving the Depression Gremlin* is most definitely a book for our times, a copy of which should be in every school in the country. For professionals working with children and young people suffering from depression it is a practical workbook that effectively offers understanding and simple practical tasks and strategies to help overcome depression and lead an emotionally healthy lifestyle. For parents, children and young people, it could be a life saver that clearly says, you are not alone and at the same time offers a wealth of knowledge that can help you to overcome that Depression Gremlin.'

– Ian Read, Headteacher, Watercliffe Meadow Primary, Sheffield

'Yet another great book that will undoubtedly help its target audience. Written in easy-to-follow language, this book will help young people to gain insight and learn to understand what is happening to their mood. With clear examples and helpful activities, this book acts as an essential instruction on how to recognise and beat the Depression Gremlin. The author has yet again written an absolute must-have book for all healthcare professionals. I am excited to share it with colleagues and to start using it in a clinical setting. I am confident this will be a "go-to" book on my shelf for years to come.'

– Dr Elizabeth Gomersall, General Practitioner

in the same series

Starving the Exam Stress Gremlin
A Cognitive Behavioural Therapy Workbook on Managing Exam Stress for Young People
Kate Collins-Donnelly
ISBN 978 1 84905 698 4
eISBN 978 1 78450 214 0

Starving the Anxiety Gremlin
A Cognitive Behavioural Therapy Workbook on Anxiety Management for Young People
Kate Collins-Donnelly
ISBN 978 1 84905 341 9
eISBN 978 0 85700 673 8

Starving the Anxiety Gremlin for Children Aged 5–9
A Cognitive Behavioural Therapy Workbook on Anxiety Management
Kate Collins-Donnelly
ISBN 978 1 84905 492 8
eISBN 978 0 85700 902 9

Starving the Anger Gremlin
A Cognitive Behavioural Therapy Workbook on Anger Management for Young People
Kate Collins-Donnelly
ISBN 978 1 84905 286 3
eISBN 978 0 85700 621 9

Starving the Anger Gremlin for Children Aged 5–9
A Cognitive Behavioural Therapy Workbook on Anger Management
Kate Collins-Donnelly
ISBN 978 1 84905 493 5
eISBN 978 0 85700 885 5

Banish Your Self-Esteem Thief
A Cognitive Behavioural Therapy Workbook on Building
Positive Self-Esteem for Young People
Kate Collins-Donnelly
ISBN 978 1 84905 462 1
eISBN 978 0 85700 841 1

Banish Your Body Image Thief
A Cognitive Behavioural Therapy Workbook on Building
Positive Body Image for Young People
Kate Collins-Donnelly
ISBN 978 1 84905 463 8
eISBN 978 0 85700 842 8

Acknowledgements

First, I would like to thank all the young people who have bravely shared their own experiences, stories, artwork, poetry and songs in this book in order to help others, as well as the young people, parents and colleagues who have given me their invaluable feedback on drafts of this book. I would also like to thank Jessica Kingsley Publishers for their ongoing support of my work. And finally, thank you to my amazing family, Maria, Nya and Finny, who are my world.

Contents

About the Author

Hi! I'm Kate, and I have worked for many years providing support for children, young people and their families on a range of emotional issues, including depression. Over the years, I have seen the debilitating effects that depression can have. But I have also witnessed the amazing recoveries that can be made by young people who courageously access appropriate avenues of treatment, support and guidance that enable them to put into practice strategies and techniques that work for them.

Hence why I wanted to write *Starving the Depression Gremlin* – a self-help workbook that aims to provide you with a better understanding of depression and how to overcome it through activities! Within its pages, you will find a wide range of tried and tested strategies, tips and tools, as well as stories from other young people to empower and inspire you to starve your Depression Gremlin and move out of the darkness that is depression.

Happy reading and good luck with starving your Depression Gremlin!

Kate

1

Why Read This Book?

Please read the following questions and colour in or tick those to which your answer is 'Yes'.

If you have answered 'Yes' to some of these questions, then this workbook is here to help you!

Starving the Depression Gremlin is a self-help workbook that contains information and activities to help you understand what depression is, why it occurs and what you can do to get it under control. It is based on three types of therapy: cognitive behavioural therapy (CBT), behavioural activation and mindfulness.

What is CBT?

CBT helps people to deal with a wide range of emotional problems, including depression, by looking at the links between our:

COGNITION

The mental processes in our minds, such as thinking and remembering

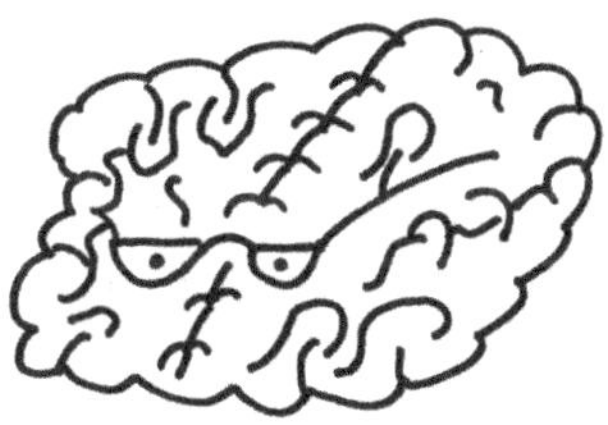

PHYSICAL REACTIONS

Things that happen in our bodies, such as feeling exhausted

EMOTIONS

Our feelings, such as scared or worried

BEHAVIOURS

How we act, such as avoiding situations or hiding away from people

What is Behavioural Activation?

Behavioural activation is based on the idea that what we do affects how we feel. It suggests that by doing more things that we enjoy, value and gain a sense of achievement from, and by reducing how much we act in negative ways, we can help to improve our mood.

What is Mindfulness?

Mindfulness originates from the spiritual discipline of Buddhism and from meditation and yoga practices. When we practise mindfulness, we make a choice to:

- become AWARE of our thoughts in the here and now without being overwhelmed by them, eaten up by them or reacting to them in a negative way
- ACCEPT that our thoughts are only thoughts and that they cannot hurt us unless we let them
- LET our thoughts GO, just like leaves blowing away in the wind.

In the chapters and activities that follow, you will learn how to apply CBT, behavioural activation and mindfulness ideas and techniques to starve your Depression Gremlin (a pesky creature that you will meet in the next chapter) and help get your depression under control!

How to Use This Workbook

The way to get the most out of *Starving the Depression Gremlin* is to work through it in its entirety. But if you want to make a quick start, please feel free to just focus on the parts that you feel are most relevant to you and your depression. And don't forget that you can always return to the other sections of the workbook in the future.

Don't worry if it all feels too hard, too much, too overwhelming or too scary at first. That is a normal way to feel when you are depressed. Some people believe that they deserve to be depressed or that they will never get better or that they are a failure for having depression. But these are not true. Others blame themselves, worry about what other people will think of them, feel embarrassed or think they are weak for not being able to cope. All these thoughts and feelings can make it hard to find the motivation to make changes, but again, none of them are true.

Depression is a very real and understandable condition, and recovery isn't just a case of 'pulling your socks up!' despite what some people may say! But we all can break the cycle of depression if we are taught how and if we remind ourselves about why we want to get better and the benefits it will bring. With the help of this workbook, you can learn how to make gradual changes to how you think and act so that improvements to your mood can be made!

Other Support Options

Exploring your depression may raise difficult issues for you. If so, please consider talking to someone you trust about these issues, such as a parent, relative, friend, teacher or mental health professional.

Please also remember that while this workbook will give you a good insight into your own depression and a vast array of information on what can help to manage it, it can still be extremely beneficial to speak to a professional, such as your GP or a psychologist, psychiatrist, counsellor or therapist, for a diagnosis and a discussion about other possible treatment options.

For some young people, if their depression is mild, this workbook may be the only help they will need. However, sometimes self-help tools alone are not enough to help a person suffering from depression make all the progress that they need to. Examples include when an individual is experiencing severe depression, or when their depression is accompanied by other mental health disorders, such as an eating disorder, or negative coping strategies like substance abuse or self-harming. In such cases, it is important to speak to your GP or psychiatrist about whether medication is appropriate and/or to seek treatment from a mental health professional. If this is the case, this workbook is suitable to be used alongside professional support.

Also, some people experiencing depression can have what we call suicidal thoughts. These are thoughts about ending your life, such as thinking life is so hopeless you don't want to continue living or thinking that others would be better off if you were dead. If you have thoughts about ending your life, it is vital that you get help straight away to keep you safe. If you have suicidal thoughts, turn to Chapter 13 now, as it looks at the types of people you can speak to for help and other ways you can keep yourself safe.

So, now that you have learnt about this workbook's purpose and basis and who it is suitable for, let's get started on starving your Depression Gremlin and overcoming your depression!

STARVING THE DEPRESSION GREMLIN STEP 1

Understanding Depression

I will soon be introducing you to an annoying creature called the Depression Gremlin. Understanding depression and how it affects you is the first big step towards starving your Depression Gremlin and getting your depression under control! Therefore, Chapters 2 to 8 of this workbook will teach you:

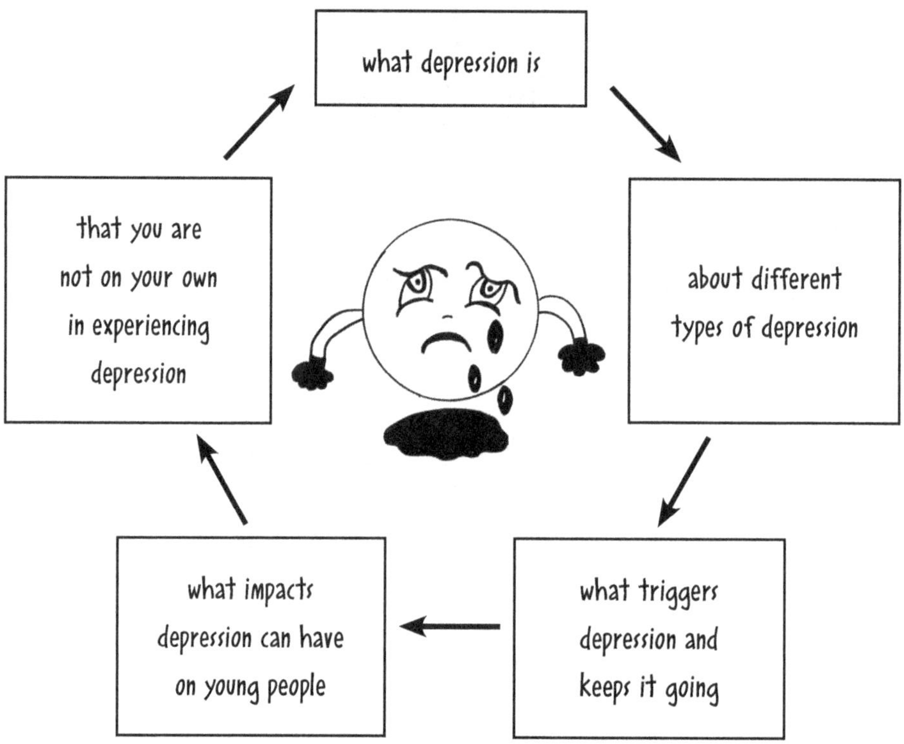

Don't forget that each bit of knowledge that you gather as you work through these chapters will help you to starve your Depression Gremlin and overcome your depression!

2

What is Depression and Who is the Depression Gremlin?

Feelings and Emotions

It is normal for everyone to experience lots of different feelings – also known as emotions – every day, such as:

You might experience some feelings more often than others or some might feel stronger than others. Some feelings might come and go quickly, whereas others might stay around for longer.

What is Depression?

Just like the other feelings mentioned above, it is also normal to feel low, sad, down, unhappy, miserable or 'blue' occasionally, especially in response to situations that are difficult in some way. But these feelings will normally go away after a short period of time when you have worked out how to respond to the situation, and your mood will go back to normal. However, if these sad feelings:

- are there most of the time (even if they are usually worse at certain times of the day, such as mornings)
- won't go away or go away but keep coming back again
- are making it really difficult for you to function in everyday life...

...then you are likely to be experiencing a form of what we call...

depression.

When we experience depression, we frequently think, feel (emotionally and physically) and act in ways that aren't good for us, such as:

- *thinking* negatively about ourselves, our lives and life events, our futures, other people and the world around us
- *feeling emotionally* like we can't enjoy things in life any more or *feeling physically* exhausted
- *acting* in ways that involve avoiding things, such as avoiding getting out of bed in the morning or avoiding certain people or situations.

The Depression Gremlin

And all of this makes a certain troublesome creature very happy. He's called the...

Depression Gremlin!

The Depression Gremlin wants you to experience depression – it's what feeds him and makes him feel full! It's what makes him grow bigger and bigger and stronger and stronger! And, as he does, your depression gets worse!

But, don't worry if your Depression Gremlin is currently massive – this workbook is here to help you starve him to get your depression under control!

In the Depression Box on the next page or on your own piece of paper, draw a picture of your Depression Gremlin and give him a name!

DEPRESSION BOX

My Depression Gremlin named. . . . .

3

Types of Depression

Mental health professionals have identified different types of depression, and learning more about them will help give you more of the knowledge you need to starve your Depression Gremlin and bring your depression under control. But please be aware that these types and their definitions can occasionally change as we learn more about depression through research. This chapter describes current categories of depression.

MAJOR DEPRESSIVE DISORDER (MDD)

This is where a young person has been experiencing five or more of the following symptoms nearly every day for at least two weeks. At least one of the symptoms must be symptom A or symptom B.

SYMPTOM A
Feeling down or irritable most of the time

SYMPTOM B
Being unable to enjoy things in life

SYMPTOM C
Tiredness or loss of energy

SYMPTOM D
Feeling worthless or guilt-ridden

SYMPTOM E
Behavioural signs of restlessness and agitation, such as pacing, fidgeting, talking quickly, wringing hands or unable to sit still, or a slowing down of movements or speech

SYMPTOM F
Significant increase or decrease in weight or appetite

SYMPTOM G
Problems thinking, concentrating or making decisions

SYMPTOM H
Not able to sleep or sleeping too much

SYMPTOM I
Suicidal thoughts or attempts

These symptoms should be causing distress or making it harder, more difficult or even impossible for the person to function as they normally would in everyday life. But they mustn't be symptoms of another physical or mental health condition or as a result of the use of a medication, illegal drug or alcohol. MDD can be classed as mild, moderate or severe and a person can have a one-off episode or it can reoccur.

There are also sub-categories of MDD that health professionals can diagnose people with. Below, I describe three of them, but there are others that haven't been discussed here.

MAJOR DEPRESSIVE DISORDER (MDD) WITH PSYCHOSIS

Some people may also have psychosis alongside their MDD. Psychosis can include:

DELUSIONS
Having unshakeable beliefs in things that aren't real or true

HALLUCINATIONS
Seeing, hearing, smelling, tasting or feeling things that appear real, but don't actually exist

MAJOR DEPRESSIVE DISORDER (MDD) WITH PERIPARTUM ONSET

This is diagnosed if a person's MDD symptoms started during pregnancy or within the first four weeks after giving birth. This is what is more commonly known as **Antenatal Depression** when it occurs during pregnancy and **Postnatal Depression** when it occurs anywhere from two weeks to two years after a woman has given birth.

MAJOR DEPRESSIVE DISORDER (MDD) WITH SEASONAL PATTERN

This is what is more commonly known as **Seasonal Affective Disorder (SAD).** It is diagnosed if a person's MDD only occurs in autumn or winter and if their mood then improves in the spring and summer when the days get longer and there is therefore more sunlight.

Other types of depression are as follows.

PERSISTENT DEPRESSIVE DISORDER (ALSO KNOWN AS 'DYSTHYMIA')

This is where a young person has experienced a depressed or irritable mood for most of the day, for more days than not, for at least a year. In addition, the young person must be experiencing at least two of the following symptoms:

Poor appetite or overeating	Not able to sleep or sleeping too much	Tiredness or low energy
Low self-esteem	Problems concentrating or making decisions	Feelings of hopelessness

The person must not be symptom free for more than two months at a time and the symptoms should be causing distress or making it harder, more difficult or even impossible for them to function as they normally would in everyday life. But they mustn't be symptoms of another physical or mental health condition or the result of the use of a medication,

illegal drug or alcohol. Like MDD, Persistent Depressive Disorder can be classed as mild, moderate or severe and can also occur during pregnancy or after giving birth or can be accompanied by psychosis.

Substance/Medication-Induced Depressive Disorder

This is where a person begins feeling down or unable to enjoy normal life pleasures and interests whilst taking or withdrawing from a substance or medication that can cause this form of side-effect. The symptoms should be causing distress or making it harder, more difficult or even impossible for the person to function as they normally would in everyday life.

Depressive Disorder Due to Another Medical Condition

This is where a person has been feeling down or has been unable to enjoy normal life pleasures and interests as a symptom of a medical condition, such as a thyroid issue, a B6 or B12 vitamin deficiency, diabetes or chronic fatigue syndrome (CFS). Again, the symptoms must be causing distress or making it harder, more difficult or even impossible for the person to function as they normally would in everyday life.

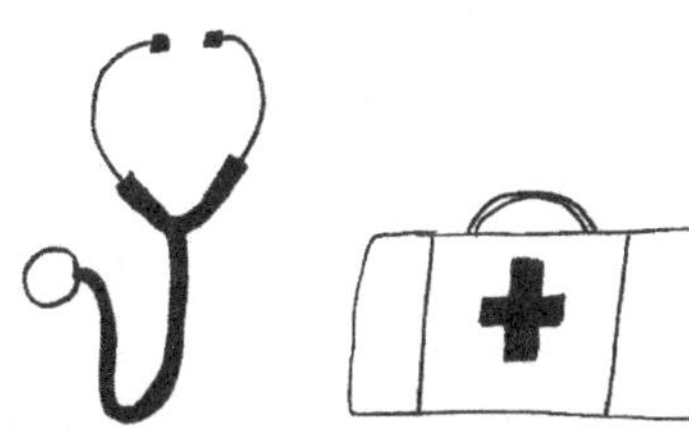

PREMENSTRUAL DYSPHORIC DISORDER

This form of depression applies to females. A female must experience at least one of the following symptoms:

- Rapid changes in emotions, such as mood swings or feeling suddenly sad or tearful
- Anger, irritability and conflicts with others
- Anxiety, tension or feeling on edge
- Depressed mood, feelings of hopelessness or negative thoughts about self

And at least one of the following symptoms:

- Change in appetite, overeating or food cravings
- Feeling overwhelmed or out of control
- Concentration problems
- Tiredness or lack of energy
- Not able to sleep or sleeping too much
- Decreased interest in usual activities
- Physical symptoms, such as breast tenderness or swelling, joint or muscle pain, bloating or weight gain

At least five symptoms must be experienced in total. They must:

* begin in the week before a menstrual period starts
* improve after the menstrual period is over

* reoccur in most menstrual cycles for a year
* be causing distress or making it harder, more difficult or even impossible for the person to function as they normally would in everyday life.

Please note, there are other types of depression that I haven't described here as I feel these would be better discussed with a healthcare professional due to their nature. These are:

- *Disruptive Mood Dysregulation Disorder* – in which symptoms are related to temper outbursts and irritability in children and young people aged 6 to 18 years
- *Other Specified Depressive Disorder or Unspecified Depressive Disorder* – one of these could be diagnosed if a person shows some signs of depression, but not enough to be diagnosed with one of the other forms of depression.

If you believe you are experiencing a form of depression, it is important to contact a healthcare or mental health professional to discuss this, especially as depression is often accompanied by other mental health issues, such as anxiety. You may find that you are diagnosed with a specific type of depression, such as one of those discussed here. But, regardless of how your depression is categorised, the information and strategies you will learn in this workbook can be of benefit to you, as we can all learn how to make improvements to our mood.

There are also other types of mental health disorders whose symptoms also include aspects of depression, such as:

- *Bipolar Disorder* – this is a mood disorder where a person switches between periods of severe depression, periods of normal mood and periods of what we call mania. Mania is where a person can feel over-excited, extremely happy, irritable, frustrated or indestructible; have lots of energy, racing thoughts and problems finishing and focusing on tasks; talk fast; and sleep very little

- *Cyclothymic Disorder* – a milder form of Bipolar Disorder.

If the symptoms of Bipolar or Cyclothymic Disorder sound like they could apply to you, please contact a healthcare or mental health professional to discuss obtaining a diagnosis and treatment options. Whilst certain strategies contained within *Starving the Depression Gremlin* may be useful to individuals suffering from either of these conditions, addressing such disorders is not the aim of this workbook.

4

What Triggers Depression?

Understanding what types of things can trigger depression can also help you to starve your Depression Gremlin and get your depression under control. Our knowledge about depression triggers continues to change and evolve as we learn more about depression through ongoing research, but what is becoming clear is how both a person's biology and their life experiences can play a part in the development of depression. So, let's look at each of these routes to depression in turn.

Route 1: Biological Triggers of Depression

The following biological factors can trigger depression in some people:

MEDICAL CONDITIONS

For some people, depression can be a symptom of certain physical conditions, such as an underactive thyroid gland or conditions that affect your blood sugar levels, such as diabetes. If you think this applies to you, it is important to discuss the relationship between your physical condition and your depression with a healthcare professional, such as your GP. They can help you decide on the best way forward for you so that you don't have to suffer.

MEDICATIONS

For some people, depression can be a side-effect of certain medications. If you have only started experiencing symptoms of depression since beginning a new medication or withdrawing from an existing medication, please check the list of side-effects in the patient information leaflet that came with the medication and speak to a healthcare professional, such as your GP, to see if there is an alternative treatment option.

SUBSTANCES

Alcohol is a depressant, which means it can have a negative effect on our mood, especially if consumed excessively. Depression can also be a side-effect of taking or withdrawing from certain illegal drugs. If you believe you have an issue with alcohol or drugs, it is important that you seek help to address this through a healthcare professional, mental health professional or support groups. Please see Appendices 1 and 2 for further information on other ways to access support.

HORMONES

Some young people may find that they experience low mood during puberty as they undergo hormonal changes in their bodies. Females may also find that their mood lowers at certain times in their menstrual cycle or whilst pregnant or after giving birth – again as a result of changes in hormone levels. If you believe this may apply to you, it is also important to speak to a healthcare professional, such as your GP, about the best ways of managing this.

SEASONS

For some people, depression can be triggered by how their body reacts to changes in the seasons each year, as discussed in the previous chapter. Treatment methods specific to this form of depression are discussed in Chapter 9 of this workbook.

Q. Do you think one of these biological factors may have triggered your depression? Please tick your answer.

YES ☐ NO ☐

Q. If yes, which one? Please tick your answer.

MEDICAL CONDITIONS ☐ MEDICATIONS ☐
SUBSTANCES ☐ HORMONES ☐ SEASONS ☐

There are two other possible biological triggers for depression. However, mental health professionals aren't presently certain as to the extent of the role they play.

DO CHEMICAL CHANGES IN THE BRAIN CAUSE DEPRESSION?

It has been suggested in the past that depression is caused by mood-related chemicals in the brain – known as neurotransmitters – being out of balance. This belief arose partly because medications used to treat depression aim to rebalance these chemicals. However, like that age-old question of what came first – the chicken or the egg – we don't actually know whether changes in brain chemicals *cause* depression or are a physical symptom that *results from* depression.

IS DEPRESSION IN OUR GENES?

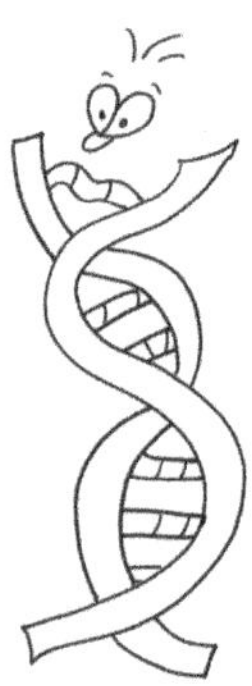

If other people in your family experience or have experienced depression, you may be more likely to develop depression yourself. However, no specific gene for depression has been identified yet. Where depression seems to 'run in families', we are learning that it may be because of the life experiences that the families share and how children can learn to react to such life experiences in the same way as their parents do, instead of it being because of something in our genetic make-up.

Route 2: Life Experiences as Triggers of Depression

Difficult, distressing or traumatic experiences can happen in life that test us emotionally, as can those that put pressure on us or those that involve loss or change. For some people, depression can be their mind and body's way of reacting to one such experience or a series of them over time. Such experiences can include:

- Neglect and abuse
- Bullying
- Family arguments/conflict
- Family illness or mental health issues
- School work or exam pressures or failing an exam
- Moving home or schools
- Pressure to be sexually active
- Homelessness
- Humiliation
- Being a carer for a family member
- Other existing or mental health issues
- Being a victim of or witnessing a crime
- Lack of love, affection or attention from parents
- Family substance misuse or alcoholism
- Physical changes during puberty
- Money worries or poverty
- Physical conditions, chronic illness, injury, pain or physical disability
- Developmental or behavioural disorders or learning disabilities
- Being taken into care
- Pressure to look a certain way
- Pressure to be successful
- Rejection, being left out by others, lack of friends or loneliness
- Parent or sibling in jail
- Being in an accident
- Parental separation or divorce
- Domestic violence
- Friendship or relationship problems
- Loss of a loved one
- Uncertainty about the future

Many of these experiences involve difficulties in our relationships with other people or how they treat us. As such, depression can also be part of our response to other people:

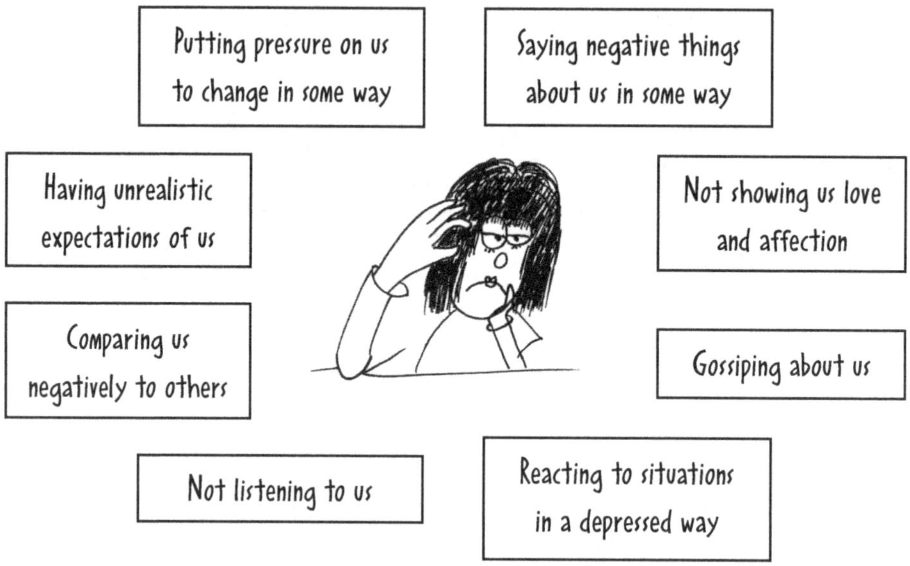

Many of the experiences we've mentioned also highlight how depression can be triggered by our basic physical needs of...

...not being met, as well as our basic psychological needs not being met, including the need to feel:

we are valued and appreciated	we are in control of our lives	our futures will be secure
our lives have meaning and purpose	we are good at something	we are liked and loved
we are understood	we are safe	we belong

In the Depression Box that follows, write down or draw pictures of any life experiences or interactions with others that may have triggered your depression. You can use any of the examples given in this chapter if they apply to you.

DEPRESSION BOX

Life experiences and interactions with others that have triggered my depression

It can feel like these life experiences and interactions with others are *making* us or *causing* us to be depressed – as though we have no control over how we respond to them emotionally. This is what the Depression Gremlin wants you to think! But if this was the case, then what would be the point in trying to manage our depression? We would just be puppets on depressed strings!

And guess who'd be holding the puppet strings...your Depression Gremlin!

But thankfully our life experiences and interactions with others don't make us become depressed. They are only ever...

triggers.

Think about it! If they caused us to be depressed, we would all become depressed in response to the same life experiences and interactions with others. But we don't!

So why not?

The next chapter will answer this question for you!

5

Our Depressed Minds

I ended the last chapter asking you why we don't all become depressed in response to the same life experiences and interactions with others. Knowing the answer to this important question will help you to starve your Depression Gremlin and get your depression under control. To help answer this question, let's meet two young people called Arianne and Finlay.

ACTING THE BULLY!

Arianne and Finlay are 15 years old and best friends. Both Arianne and Finlay have dyslexia. It doesn't bother them much at school as they get extra help when they need it and they work hard and achieve good grades. They both enjoy school and get on well with the other pupils in their year group at school.

Both Arianne and Finlay love singing and acting and go to a performing arts club twice a week. Sometimes, they mix up words when performing on stage because of their dyslexia. Two other young people in their performing arts club, Jess and Andrew, have laughed at them and said mean things to them about it when it has happened.

Since Arianne and Finlay were given the lead roles in an upcoming musical, Jess and Andrew have started writing mean things about them and their dyslexia on social media.

Arianne

Arianne cannot stop thinking about what Jess and Andrew have been writing about her and wonders if their words are true. All day, every day, negative thoughts whiz around Arianne's head, such as 'I am going to mix up my words on opening night and the audience will laugh at me. I am a failure, stupid and useless, and my dream of becoming an actress will never come true.' She has now pulled out of the lead role in the musical because she believes that 'there is no point as I am too stupid to remember my lines properly'. She has started to spend most of her free time in bed as she is not motivated to do anything else. She doesn't speak to other pupils at school any more, including Finlay, as she thinks that 'my friends will all laugh at me when I speak'. She now thinks that 'school is pointless, and my life is hopeless'. Arianne doesn't enjoy life any more, feels down and tired most of the time, frequently skips classes at school and struggles to sleep or eat.

Finlay

Finlay is upset about Jess and Andrew's mean comments. However, he thinks, 'They are the ones with the problem, not me, as we all have a right to be treated with respect.' His thoughts focus on what he knows to be true, such as 'dyslexia doesn't make me stupid', 'I do well at school,' and 'I am good at acting'. He also thinks, 'I'm proud of me and my achievements, and the things they are writing about me aren't true, so I just have to ignore them.' Finlay reports the behaviour of Jess and Andrew to the performing arts teacher, stops going on social media and turns up to every rehearsal excited to perform.

Both Arianne and Finlay are going through the exact same life experience and interactions with others – bullying by Jess and Andrew. Arianne is showing signs of depression in response to the bullying, but Finlay isn't.

Q. Why is this?

....

....

If you found it difficult to answer this question, looking at each of their thoughts should help.

Arianne: 'I am going to mix up my words on opening night and the audience will laugh at me. I am a failure, stupid and useless, and my dream of becoming an actress will never come true.' 'I am too stupid to remember my lines properly.' 'My friends will all laugh at me when I speak.' 'School is pointless and my life is hopeless.'

Finlay: 'They are the ones with the problem, not me, as we all have a right to be treated with respect.' 'Dyslexia doesn't make me stupid.' 'I do well at school.' 'I am good at acting.' 'I'm proud of me and my achievements, and the things they are writing about me aren't true, so I just have to ignore them.'

Finlay isn't experiencing signs of depression in response to the bullying as he is...

thinking differently

...from Arianne about the life experience that they are going through.

It is how we...

think about our life experiences and interactions with others

...and how that leads us to...

think about ourselves, our lives and life events, our futures, other people and the world around us

...that can lead to us feeling depressed, not the life experiences and interactions themselves.

Finlay is thinking positively and realistically and, as a result, can keep his mood more positive and act in constructive ways to address the situation. However, Arianne is thinking negatively and unrealistically about herself, her abilities, her life and her future in response to the situation and is predicting worst-case scenarios that are unlikely to occur. Arianne is thinking through her...

Depression Thinking Glasses!

And this is causing her to feel depressed.

What are Depression Thinking Glasses?

Here are some common types of Depression Thinking Glasses:

MAGNIFYING GLASSES

When you think through these glasses everything seems bigger, worse, more important or more dangerous than it actually is!

For example, when 16-year-old Clayton's girlfriend ends their relationship, he thinks, 'My life is over now.'

When thinking through these glasses you may also make assumptions about yourself, your life and life events, your future and the world or people in general based on one event.

For example, Fiona, aged 13 years, thinks that 'all people are horrible' when one person in her class says something mean to her.

MAKE BELIEVE GLASSES

When you think through these glasses you imagine things to be true even though you don't know whether they are true or not! This can involve jumping to a lot of conclusions about things.

For example, when Zara doesn't say hello to her friend Kara, aged 14 years, in the street, Kara thinks that 'it's because she hates me' when it was actually because Zara didn't see her.

FORTUNE TELLING GLASSES

When you think through these glasses you predict that bad things will happen in the future! Your predictions often involve worst-case scenarios and failure and you think bad things are more likely to happen than they actually are!

For example, when Jarrod, aged 15 years, fails a mock exam, he thinks, 'I will fail all my real exams and my parents will hate me.'

DOOM AND GLOOM GLASSES

When you think through these glasses you only pay attention to things about you, your life and life events or the world and people around you that are negative. You also see the worst in everything, think that everything is wrong or will go wrong and that anything that goes wrong will be the end of the world!

For example, when her best friend moves schools, Sonia, aged 11 years, thinks, 'I have no-one now. I can't go back to school as I'm all alone.'

MIND READING GLASSES

When you think through these glasses you imagine what other people are thinking – usually negative things about you – even though you don't actually know what they are thinking!

For example, Nisha, aged 12 years, thinks, 'Everyone at school believes I'm weird and ugly.'

WHAT IF? GLASSES

When you think through these glasses you ask yourself, 'What if this bad thing happens?' or 'What if that bad thing happens?' even though they are unlikely to happen!

For example, Darius, aged 12 years, is always thinking, 'What if people laugh at me?' whenever he has to speak or do something in front of other people.

ALL OR NOTHING GLASSES

When you think through these glasses you think in extremes or in 'black and white' ways, such as things are either great or awful. There is no in between or 'shades of grey'.

For example, Cate, aged 14 years, thinks, 'If I can't get 100% in my maths test, I shouldn't bother trying at all.'

UNHAPPY MEMORIES GLASSES

When you think through these glasses you are more likely to remember unhappy memories and forget the happy ones.

For example, even though Francesca, aged 13 years, has won lots of cross-country races, she cannot stop thinking about the time she came last.

I'M USELESS GLASSES

When you think through these glasses you put yourself down and compare yourself negatively to others!

For example, Kristina, aged 14 years, thinks, 'Everyone is more beautiful and cleverer than me. I'm a worthless nobody.'

SELF-BLAME GLASSES

When you think through these glasses you blame yourself for everything negative that happens in life and take the actions of others personally.

For example, Mario, aged 10 years, thinks, 'My mum has cancer because I've been so naughty at home and school.'

I SHOULD GLASSES

When you think through these glasses you think you should be perfect at things and not make mistakes. You also think that if you're not perfect, bad things will happen or that you're not good enough or that people won't like or love you. You can also spend a lot of time thinking that things in your life should be better than they are.

For example, Greg, aged 15 years, thinks, 'If I'm not perfect at everything in life, no-one will like me.'

I CAN'T GLASSES

When you think through these glasses you think you can't do things even though you can! You can also see yourself as helpless or trapped and you can see any difficult or unpleasant situations or feelings as too much for you to cope with.

For example, Nelson, aged 16 years, thinks, 'I can't go to college. I'm not good enough. It will be too hard. I won't cope and I'll fail.'

WHAT'S THE POINT? GLASSES

When you think through these glasses life seems hopeless and pointless and suicidal thoughts are more likely.

For example, Oscar, aged 16 years, thinks, 'There's no point to me or my life. I'm a useless and worthless waste of space.'

MY FEELINGS ARE FACTS GLASSES

When you think through these glasses you view how you feel emotionally as reality – i.e. "I feel it, so it must be true."

For example, Tess, aged 12 years, thinks, 'I feel like everything is hopeless, so it must be, and I feel like a failure, so I must be.'

IGNORING THE GOOD GLASSES

When you think through these glasses you ignore the positives about you, your life or situations or twist them into negatives in some way.

For example, Wes, aged 11 years, thinks, 'My adoptive parents are only nice to me because they feel sorry for me.'

In the Depression Box on the next page, write down any overly negative or unrealistic thoughts you frequently have about yourself, your life and your future. Also write down any overly negative or unrealistic thoughts you frequently have about other people and the world around you. Then write down which type of Depression Thinking Glasses you are wearing for each thought. Be aware that sometimes our thoughts can be in the form of images in our minds.

DEPRESSION BOX

THOUGHTS ABOUT ME, MY LIFE AND MY FUTURE	TYPE OF DEPRESSION THINKING GLASSES
THOUGHTS ABOUT OTHER PEOPLE AND THE WORLD AROUND ME	TYPE OF DEPRESSION THINKING GLASSES

Depression Thinking

Because it is how we...

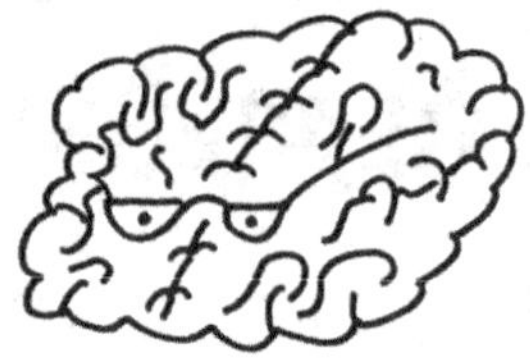

think about our life experiences and interactions with others

...that leads us to have a depressed reaction, the Depression Gremlin wants us to wear our Depression Thinking Glasses all the time, like Arianne.

He wants us to think:

- that life experiences and interactions with others are worse than they actually are – blowing them out of proportion
- that there is no way to cope and that, if we can't cope, then we are failures
- negatively and unrealistically about ourselves, our lives and our futures as well as about other people and the world around us.

Why?

Because the Depression Gremlin wants us to be depressed. He wants us to feel down, bleak and hopeless! Remember, it's what feeds him!

Even when our depression has a biological trigger (see Chapter 4), how we think whilst feeling depressed can also feed our Depression Gremlin, making our depression worse and keeping us trapped in its vicious cycle. For example, Sophie, aged 16 years, has depression that is triggered by her hormones. But Sophie's depression is worsening, as she is constantly thinking that her life is horrible because of how awful she feels whenever she has a period and that she will never be able to be happy in the future.

So, the more we think in overly negative and unrealistic ways about ourselves, our lives and life events, our futures, other people and the world around us using our Depression Thinking Glasses, the more we...

feed our Depression Gremlin

...making him bigger and bigger and fuller and fuller...

...and us more and more depressed!

And the more depressed we get, the harder and harder it is to take our Depression Thinking Glasses off and depressed thoughts get stuck in our heads just like the picture below by Anya, aged 12 years shows.

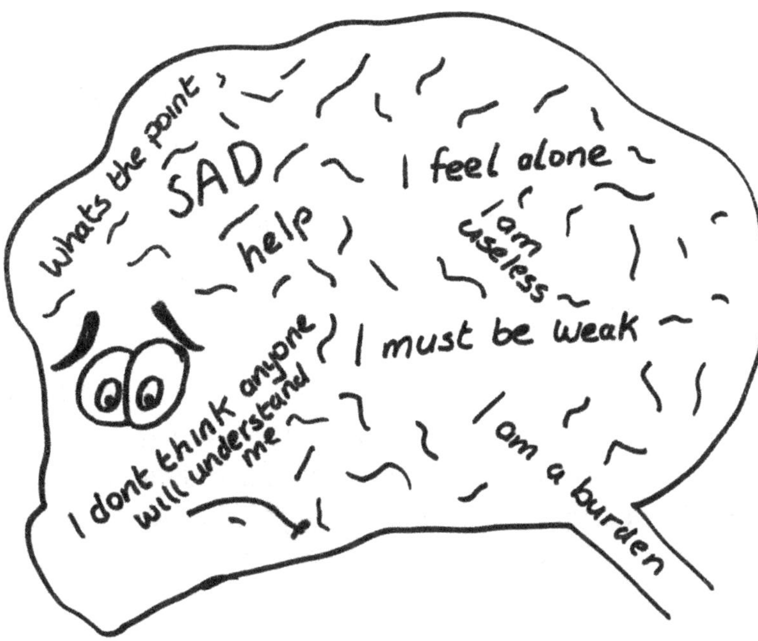

By Anya, aged 12 years

They play over and over again in our minds just like a song on repeat on our mobile phones!

And we cannot stop thinking about them. We call this...

ruminating.

Ruminating can lead to deep-rooted beliefs that we believe in 100% and guide how we think about every situation we experience and how we choose to live our lives. For example, 15-year-old Gwen's beliefs are:

'I'm unloveable' (about herself)	**'Life is rubbish'** (about life)	**'I'll be lonely forever'** (about her future)
'No-one likes me' (about others)	**'The world is a horrible place'** (about the world)	

Some people experiencing depression will also have thoughts about their life not being worth living, about people or the world being better off without them and/or about harming themselves or ending their lives. If you experience these thoughts, please turn to Chapter 13 immediately, where I discuss a plan that can help to keep you safe and address such thoughts.

When we frequently think negatively and unrealistically as part of the cycle of depression, it can affect our brain's ability to function in other ways too. The boxes that follow contain things that our brains can find it hard to do when we are depressed. Colour in or tick any that apply to you.

- Following processes or sequences, such as a recipe
- Concentrating, focusing and paying attention
- Making decisions
- Understanding information (we call this 'comprehension')
- Remembering things
- Reading
- Gathering thoughts into a logical and clear format
- Putting thoughts down on paper or saying them out loud in a clear and reasoned way

All of these can make it harder for us to function in our everyday lives, which in turn helps to keep us stuck in the vicious cycle of depression. Experiencing these other cognitive symptoms worsens our thinking patterns and our Depression Gremlin gets even bigger and our depression worsens!

This constant negative and unrealistic thinking can lead to us feeling bad physically and emotionally and acting in ways that hinder us further – thus keeping us trapped in a vicious cycle of depression – as you will see in the next chapter.

6

Our Depressed Minds, Bodies, Emotions and Behaviours

What Keeps Depression Going?

Understanding what keeps depression going will also help you to starve your Depression Gremlin and get your depression under control. Let's look at this using something called the Depression Gremlin Cycle.

The Depression Gremlin Cycle

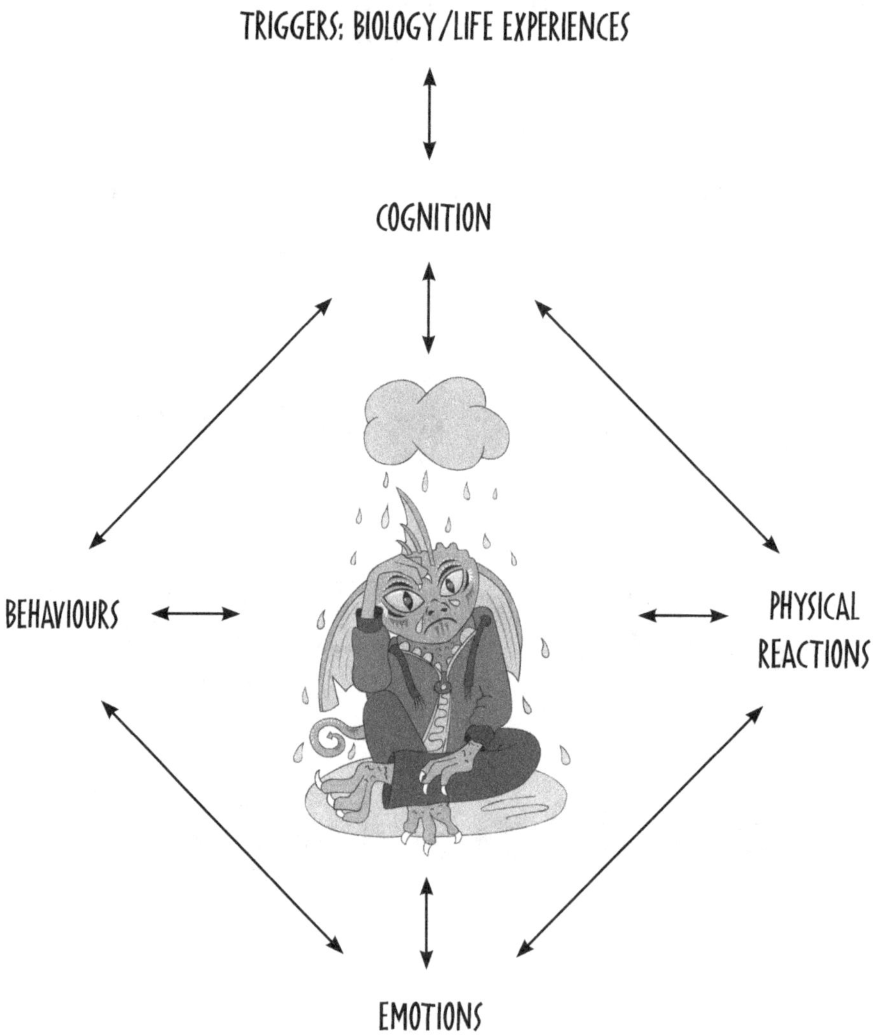

The Depression Gremlin Cycle is based on a cognitive behavioural approach. It highlights how depression is maintained due to an interaction between the trigger(s) and our...

COGNITION

The mental processes in our minds, such as thinking and remembering

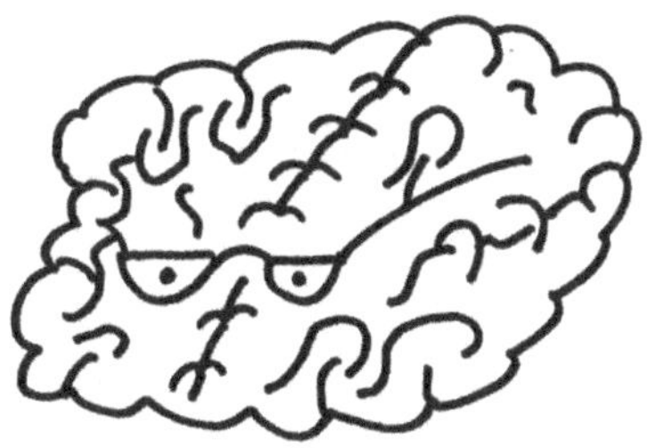

PHYSICAL REACTIONS

Things that happen in our bodies, such as feeling exhausted

EMOTIONS

Our feelings, such as scared or worried

BEHAVIOURS

How we act, such as avoiding situations or hiding away from people

The cycle shows that it is how we...

think about ourselves, our lives and life events, our futures, other people and the world around us

...that affects:

- our brain's ability to function in other ways, such as remembering things
- how our bodies react physically
- how we feel emotionally
- how we then choose to behave.

So, let's look at each part of the cycle with the help of a 12-year-old boy called Logan who has depression.

Cognition

The first part of the Depression Gremlin Cycle recaps what we learnt in the previous chapter – namely:

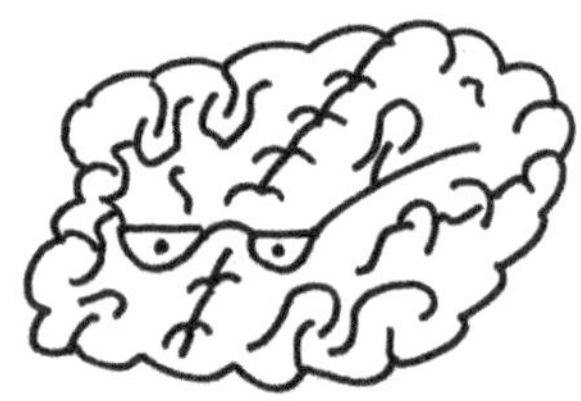

- If we think overly negatively and unrealistically about ourselves, our lives and life events, our futures, other people and the world around us using our Depression Thinking Glasses, we feed our Depression Gremlin and experience depression.
- And the more we feed our Depression Gremlin, the more likely we are to continue to think negatively and unrealistically – thus feeding our Depression Gremlin some more and helping to keep our depression going!
- And the harder it is for our brains to function in other ways, such as remembering things.
- And the more we feed our Depression Gremlin, the bigger and bigger he gets and the more depressed we are likely to be!

Logan's frequent depressed thoughts are a good example of feeding a Depression Gremlin by thinking negatively and unrealistically, as you will see from the picture below.

Physical Reactions

The Depression Gremlin Cycle also shows that when we frequently think negatively and unrealistically as part of our depression, we can trigger off negative physical reactions in our bodies, such as feeling tired all the time.

Logan's physical reactions include loss of appetite, feeling sick and exhausted all the time, headaches, and stomach and muscle aches.

The more we experience negative physical reactions like Logan, the more we feed our Depression Gremlin, the bigger and bigger he gets and the more and more depressed we become.

In the Depression Box on the next page are a range of negative physical reactions that we can experience when we are depressed. Colour in or tick any that apply to you and your depression.

DEPRESSION BOX

- HEADACHES
- CONSTANT TIREDNESS OR LACK OF ENERGY
- FEELING RUN DOWN
- SPEECH THAT IS SLOWER THAN USUAL
- UNEXPLAINED MUSCLE PAINS OR ACHES OR BEING MORE SENSITIVE TO PAIN
- NAUSEA
- LOSS OR CHANGE OF APPETITE
- STOMACH CHURNING OR ACHE
- CONSTIPATION OR DIARRHOEA
- CHANGES TO MENSTRUAL CYCLE
- WEIGHT LOSS OR GAIN
- MOVEMENT THAT IS SLOWER THAN USUAL

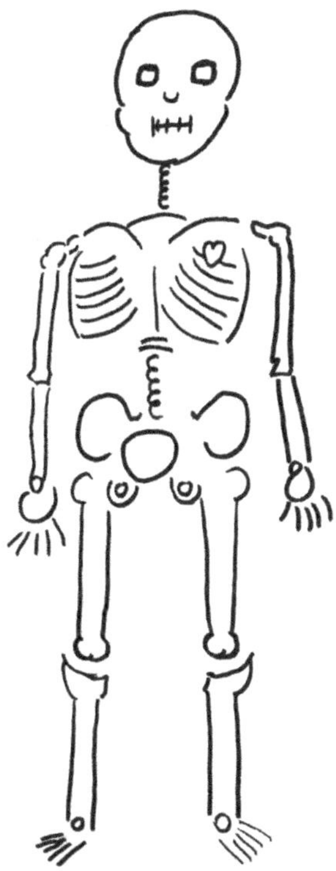

- SLEEP DISTURBANCE, INCLUDING DIFFICULTIES GETTING TO SLEEP, WAKING FREQUENTLY, NIGHTMARES OR EXCESSIVE SLEEPING

Physical reactions

Emotions

The Depression Gremlin Cycle also shows that when we frequently think negatively and unrealistically as part of our depression, we can trigger off other negative emotions.

For Logan, this involves feeling:

Sense of despair

Sad

Overwhelmed

Lonely

Ashamed

Miserable

Hopeless

Helpless

Empty

The more we experience these other negative emotions, the more we feed our Depression Gremlin, the bigger he gets and the more depressed we become.

In the Depression Box on the next page are a range of negative emotions that we can experience as part of depression. Colour in or tick any that apply to you and your depression.

DEPRESSION BOX

Sadness	Low mood	Miserableness
Loss of motivation or interest	Loss of pleasure or enjoyment	Feeling worthless
Feeling fed up	Agitation or restlessness	Despair
Guilt	Loneliness or isolation	Frustration
Emptiness	Anxiety, worry, nervousness or panic	Unhappiness
Feeling overwhelmed	Self-doubt	Hopelessness
Helplessness	Shame	Irritability
Dread or fear	Self-loathing	Upset or distress
Low in confidence	Feeling trapped	Defensiveness
Numbness	Humiliation	Feeling uncertain
Sense of inadequacy or inferiority	Insecurity	Disappointment
Sense of darkness or bleakness	Loss of sense of humour	Stress or pressure
		Anger

Emotions

Behaviours

Finally, the Depression Gremlin Cycle shows that the more we think in negative and unrealistic ways and experience negative physical reactions and emotions, the more likely it is that we will start acting in ways that aren't good for us, such as avoiding situations, which feeds our Depression Gremlin further, making him bigger and bigger and us more and more depressed!

In the Depression Box on the next two pages is a list of ways in which people can act when they are experiencing depression. Tick any that you do regularly because of your depression.

DEPRESSION BOX

BEHAVIOUR	APPLIES TO ME
Avoid or escape from certain situations	
Waste time doing other activities instead of the activities you should be doing	
Quit/give up part way through activities	
Give up on activities before you've even tried	
Put off doing certain activities/procrastinate	
Stop doing things you used to do, including things you used to enjoy and be interested in	
Reduce activity levels in general	
Loss of routine	
Stop laughing	
Avoid making decisions or solving problems	
Avoid leaving your bed, bedroom or the house	
Hide away from people, such as stopping going out with or playing with friends	
Neglect personal appearance or physical hygiene	
Hide how you are feeling from other people	
Act angrily towards yourself	

BEHAVIOUR	APPLIES TO ME
Act aggressively or irritably towards others	
Argue with others	
Take your feelings out on others	
Break off a relationship or friendship	
Act in defensive ways	
Act in defiant or non-compliant ways	
Act in disruptive ways	
Put yourself down or criticise yourself when you speak	
Cry	
Skip meals	
Binge or comfort eat	
Make yourself sick after eating	
Drink or take drugs	
Refuse to go to school	
Do things that get you into trouble or commit risk-taking behaviours, such as stealing or truancy	
Self-harm, which involves deliberately hurting or injuring yourself, such as by cutting, scratching, hitting or burning yourself	
Act in ways to get people's attention	
Seek reassurance from others	
Stay close to a certain person or people as much as possible, such as not wanting to be apart from your mum	

BEHAVIOUR	APPLIES TO ME
Become dependent on other people, such as needing others to do certain things for you	
Need items as a comfort, such as a favourite soft toy or a 'lucky charm'	
Act in restless ways, such as pacing, fidgeting or difficulties sitting still	
Talk faster or slower	
Suicide attempts	

Behaviours

We often act in the ways listed in the previous Depression Box because we think they will bring short-term benefits. For example, some young people self-harm because it temporarily provides:

- a way of coping with, relieving or distracting from painful, distressing or unpleasant thoughts and feelings
- a way of feeling something if they usually feel numb
- a sense of control when everything else feels out of control
- a way of punishing themselves or turning anger towards themselves.

Other young people might use alcohol or illegal drugs as a way of:

- forgetting about life problems
- coping with or distracting from painful, distressing or unpleasant feelings
- boosting confidence to face situations.

However, these behaviours actually have negative impacts on us in both the short and long term, and, as a result, we call them...

self-defeating behaviours.

For example, drinking alcohol can help to lower a person's mood and, in some cases, can make people more susceptible to anger, irritability and aggression. And both alcohol and drugs can upset the balance of chemicals in a person's brain, which is especially dangerous for young people as their brains are still developing. They can also be addictive, making people feel like they cannot cope without more of them. They can also affect decision-making, make it harder to think clearly and to function in everyday life, make acting in risky ways more likely, cause hallucinations (where you see or hear things that aren't real), cause confusion and edginess, and increase suicidal thoughts.

Logan's self-defeating behaviours are...

- refusing to go to school
- quitting all after-school clubs
- staying at home in bed all the time
- no longer contacting his friends
- stopping any exercise
- not eating much
- not showering

As a result, he has lost a considerable amount of weight, hates himself when he looks in the mirror, and feels even more empty, miserable, worthless, ashamed and unmotivated.

The more self-defeating our behaviours become, the more we feed our Depression Gremlin and the more depressed we become.

Plus:

- the worse we feel physically and emotionally
- the harder we find it to perform the mental processes needed to function effectively in everyday life
- the more negative and unrealistic thoughts we have about ourselves, our lives and life events, our futures, others and the world around us.

In addition, self-defeating behaviours prevent us from:

- seeing that the bad things we worry about happening are unlikely to happen and that even if they did we would cope with them
- finding out how differently we could think and feel if we didn't behave in these ways
- finding out that the assumptions we make aren't realistic or accurate
- discovering more constructive and positive ways to cope with situations and our depression.

The result...we end up stuck in the middle of a very vicious cycle of depression. And it is this never-ending cycle of negative cognition, physical reactions, emotions and behaviours that keeps depression going by feeding your Depression Gremlin – enabling him to get bigger and bigger and your depression worse and worse!

And this can lead to a whole host of other negative impacts on us and our lives, as we will see in the next chapter.

7

Impacts of Depression

Think about your own experience of depression and write down in the Depression Box below the negative impacts you think it has had on you and your life. Again, understanding what these impacts have been for you will help you to starve your Depression Gremlin and overcome your depression.

DEPRESSION BOX

Impacts of depression on me and my life

You may have talked about the impacts your depression has had on your:

- physical health
- mental health and emotional wellbeing
- relationships
- academic achievements
- social and leisure activities, and/or
- goals for the future.

PHYSICAL HEALTH

As our bodies can release stress hormones and our immune systems can weaken when we are depressed, impacts on our physical health can include:

* becoming more susceptible to illness and infections
* making current illnesses, allergies or pain levels worse
* our bodies being less effective at healing, such as when repairing tissue damage
* vaccinations being less effective.

We can also experience:

* negative physical effects as a result of behaviours that aren't good for us health wise, such as severe weight loss and a lack of energy from under-eating
* the other physical reactions in our bodies that we discussed in Chapter 6.

MENTAL HEALTH AND EMOTIONAL WELLBEING

Impacts on our mental health and emotional wellbeing can include:

* developing other emotional and mental health conditions alongside depression, such as anxiety, stress, obsessive compulsive disorder (OCD), phobias, addictions and eating disorders
* experiencing any of the other negative emotions discussed in Chapter 6
* developing low self-esteem, and a lack of self-confidence and self-belief
* losing our sense of identity – i.e. who we are as a person
* difficulties experiencing positive emotions, such as excitement and joy
* a reduced sense of pleasure, enjoyment, happiness levels and life satisfaction
* problems coping with change or with difficult, challenging or new situations
* using negative coping strategies, such as self-harming and substance misuse
* feeling like life is not worth living and suicidal thoughts.

RELATIONSHIPS

Various stresses, strains and pressures can occur in our relationships with family, friends, boyfriends/girlfriends and other important people in our lives if, as a result of depression, we:

* withdraw from interacting socially with others
* seek constant reassurance or attention from others
* take our emotions out on others
* act in negative ways towards others, such as aggression
* focus so much on our own negative thoughts and feelings that we ignore or neglect the needs and feelings of others
* have a lack of confidence and self-belief
* have a belief that we will disappoint others or they will no longer like us or love us if we don't meet what we believe to be their high expectations of us
* have overly negative and unrealistic thoughts and beliefs about ourselves, our lives and life events, our futures, other people and the world around us.

The above factors can make it harder for us to maintain existing relationships and also to start new ones, and can lead us to feel isolated from others socially. People close to us can also be worried about us because of our depression, which can also impact on those relationships.

ACADEMIC ACHIEVEMENTS

Depression can hinder our performance academically because it can involve cognitive difficulties, including difficulties with:

* memory
* concentration, focus and attention
* understanding information (what we call 'comprehension')
* following processes or sequences
* gathering our thoughts into a logical and clear format
* reading
* putting our thoughts down on paper or saying them out loud in a reasoned and clear way
* making decisions.

When we are depressed we can also:

* lack confidence and doubt our abilities
* think overly negatively and unrealistically about ourselves and our studies
* lack the interest or motivation needed to attend lessons or complete homework
* avoid school or specific lessons or exams
* put off doing homework
* avoid speaking in class.

All of these can disrupt our learning, and lead us to make more mistakes, which in turn hinders our ability to demonstrate our true knowledge and skills in lessons, assignments and exams.

SOCIAL AND LEISURE ACTIVITIES

Depression can prevent us from living life to the full as we can:

* lose interest in things we used to enjoy
* lose the motivation, energy or confidence to do things we used to enjoy or to try new things
* find it difficult to experience pleasure and enjoyment in life
* start to dread each day or certain activities
* feel like activities take too much effort
* stop wanting to be around other people
* doubt ourselves and our abilities and be afraid of failure or things going wrong
* believe that doing things is pointless or hopeless or that life isn't worth living anyway.

GOALS FOR THE FUTURE

Depression and all its various symptoms and effects can combine to have a major impact on our:

* interest in and motivation to achieve our future goals and desires
* belief in our ability to achieve them
* actual ability to achieve them.

It can also lead us to have very few goals and desires in the first place.

All these negative impacts feed our Depression Gremlin further – making him bigger and bigger and keeping us stuck in that vicious cycle of depression. But, please don't be disheartened by this! It's possible to break out of this vicious cycle, starve your Depression Gremlin and manage your depression, as the rest of this workbook will show!

8

You're Not on Your Own in Experiencing Depression

Another step towards starving your Depression Gremlin and overcoming your depression is to realise you are not on your own in experiencing depression. Researchers have asked children and young people about depression through face-to-face interviews and online and paper surveys. The research examples that you will read about in the following newspaper – *The Depression Gazette* – clearly highlight that you are not on your own, as depression affects many children and young people today.

The Depression Gazette

Young People and Mental Health

Mental health issues can affect anyone – no matter what their age, gender, ethnicity, sexuality, social background, etc. But research shows that 50% of mental health problems are established by the age of 14 (Kessler *et al.* 2005) and 75% by the age of 18 (Kim-Cohen *et al.* 2003).

How Many Young People are Affected?

The World Health Organization (2003) estimates that, every year, 20% of adolescents across the globe may experience a mental health problem, with rates among young people in prisons (Office for National Statistics 1997) and the care system (NICE 2010; Sempik, Ward and Darker 2008), and among young carers (Sempik and Becker 2013), young people in gangs (Coid *et al.* 2013), young people from the poorest households (Chief Medical Officer 2014) and young people who have been bullied (Lereya *et al.* 2013) being even higher.

In the UK

According to figures quoted by the charity MQ (2016), less than 30% of the total mental health research spend in the UK is put towards studies on the mental health of children and young people. But, what *do* we know?

The Depression Gazette Page 1

Well, the first official statistics to be published in 13 years (Sadler *et al.* 2018), based on a national survey of children and young people in England, show that:

- 9.5% of 5- to 10-year olds, 14.4% of 11- to 16-year olds and 16.9% of 17- to 19-year olds have at least one mental health disorder.
- Emotional disorders, such as anxiety or depression, were the most common type of disorder experienced by 5- to 19-year olds.
- Boys aged 5 to 10 years were more likely to have a mental health disorder than girls of the same age, and between 11 to 16 years of age, both sexes were equally as likely to have a mental health disorder.
- Girls aged 17 to 19 years were more than twice as likely to have a disorder than boys, with one in four girls in this age range suffering. In addition, over half of those girls reported having self-harmed or attempted suicide.
- Young people who identified as LGBT were more likely to have a mental health disorder (34.9%) than those who identified as heterosexual (13.2%).
- Approximately 11% of young people aged 11 to 19 years had low self-esteem.
- Young people aged 11 to 19 years with a mental health disorder were nearly twice as likely (59.1%) to have been bullied in the past year than those without a disorder.
- School exclusions, risky health behaviours such as substance misuse, self-harming and suicide attempts were also more likely in children and young people experiencing a mental health disorder.

Another recent national survey of children's wellbeing revealed that almost 25% displayed signs of mental ill health, including anxiety and depression (Office for National Statistics 2016), and an international study of the life satisfaction of children aged 10 to 12 years in 15 countries ranked England 14 out of 15 (Rees and Main 2015).

Furthermore, in 2016–17, 50% of all counselling sessions conducted by ChildLine related to mental and emotional health issues (NSPCC 2017), a British Psychological Society survey of mental health providers found that 89% had reported increases in referrals for children and young people (House of Commons Health Committee 2014) and approximately 1 in 250 children were referred to the Child and Adolescent Mental Health Service (CAMHS) in the UK in 2015.

However, on average, 28% of those referred to CAMHS were turned away without being offered help. This figure was as high as 75% in some areas of the country (Children's Commissioner 2016) and Frith (2016) found that the average maximum waiting time for a first appointment with CAMHS was 6 months and nearly 10 months until the start of treatment.

The Depression Gazette Page 2

Similar findings were reported by Sadler *et al.* (2018), with the survey finding that one in five young people with a mental health disorder had waited more than six months for contact with a mental health specialist. In addition, Burstow and Jenkins (2016) found that only 25% of children needing treatment receive it and a survey of headteachers in the UK in 2016 found that 65% struggled to get mental health support for pupils (London School of Economics 2015). And according to the 2015-16 Young Minds annual report (Young Minds 2016), less than 1% of the NHS budget is in fact spent on children's mental health – equating to £78 per child aged 0 to 17 years.

A YouGov survey on behalf of the charity MQ found that 56% of young people thought that if someone their age was to develop a condition they would be worried about being treated differently. In addition, 55% felt that they would be worried about losing friends, 51% about feeling embarrassed and 49% about never getting better (YouGov/MQ and Forster 2016).

An annual Girl Guides Girls' Attitudes Survey found in 2015 that 58% of 13- to 21-year-olds believed mental health to be one of the biggest worries in their lives, with an increasing number seeing depression and self-harm as the most significant health issues facing their age group. Sixty-two per cent knew a girl their age who had experienced a mental health problem, but 57% stated that they felt awkward talking about mental health (Girl Guides Association 2015).

In a 2016 survey for Parent Zone, 93% of teachers reported seeing increased rates of mental health issues among children and teenagers and 90% thought the issues were getting more severe (Rosen 2016).

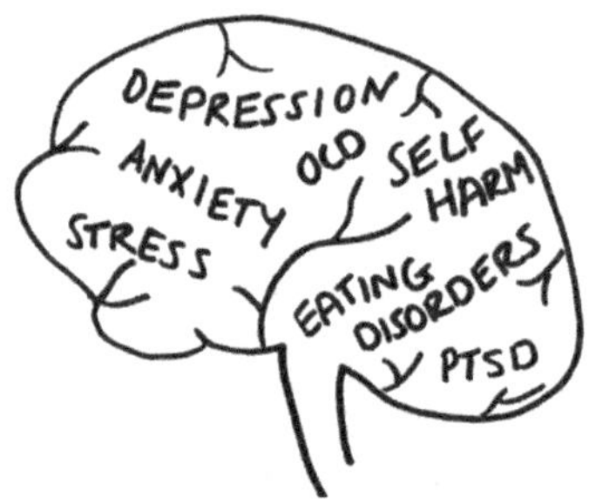

Depression Affects Many

According to the World Health Organization (2017), 322 million people are living with depression worldwide, which is an increase of over 18% between 2005 and 2015.

Young People and Depression

On the Increase!

Studies worldwide show increasing levels of depression among children and young people (e.g. Mental Health Foundation 2004; Mojtabai, Olfson and Han 2016; Nuffield Foundation 2013), with many showing that the risk of developing

The Depression Gazette Page 3

depression increases significantly in adolescence (e.g. Avenevoli *et al.* 2015; Merikangas *et al.* 2010; Public Health England 2016). The World Health Organization (2014) describes depression as the leading cause of illness and disability in young people. Furthermore, the latest Good Childhood Report (Children's Society 2018) found that children's happiness is the lowest it has been since 2010 and, of those children and young people who had low happiness with life, 47% also had high depressive symptoms, with 11% reporting high depressive symptoms overall.

In the UK

The recent national survey of children and young people's mental health in England (Sadler *et al.* 2018) found that 2.1% of children and young people were experiencing a depressive disorder, with this increasing to 4.8% for young people aged 17 to 19 years. According to YoungMinds (2011), 2% of children and young people under the age of 12 experience depression and 5% of young people aged 13 years and over.

In 2013–14, the ChildLine website pages on 'Depression and feeling sad' received approximately 52,000 views and their video on depression was viewed more than 24,000 times (NSPCC 2014a). In the same year, young people stated that they were depressed in 56% of ChildLine's counselling sessions that related to mental health – this equated to 7194 counselling sessions; and they stated they were feeling suicidal in 20% of the sessions – a rise of 116% compared to 2010–11 (NSPCC 2014a, 2014b).

In 2016–17, the top concern raised by young people who contacted ChildLine was mental and emotional health issues, including depression and suicidal thoughts (NSPCC 2017).

Statistics from a YouGov survey of university students published in 2016 found that over a quarter of university students report having a mental health problem, with over three-quarters of these suffering with depression (YouGov 2016). Similar findings were obtained using data gained from the UK Household Longitudinal Survey in 2014–15, where 19% of young people aged 16 to 24 years were found to have symptoms of anxiety or depression (Office for National Statistics 2017).

Worldwide

A national survey in Australia revealed that 1 in 16 young people are currently experiencing depression (Australian Bureau of Statistics 2008), and a survey by Mission Australia (2018) found that when asked about their happiness levels, approximately 28% of young Australians are 'unhappy or sad' and a further 10% are very sad.

The Depression Gazette Page 4

In America, a report by the Centers for Disease Control and Prevention (2013) estimated that 2.1% of 3- to 17-year-olds had a current diagnosis of depression. Another American study by Breslau *et al.* (2017) found that depression can start as early as age 11 for many young people, and that approximately 14% of boys and 36% of girls had experienced depression by 17 years of age. The 2018 State of Mental Health in America report (Nguyen *et al.* 2018) found that rates of severe depression in 12- to 17-year-olds had risen from 5.9% to 8.2% in a five-year period. Furthermore, approximately 12% report suffering from at least one major depression episode in the past year, and 63% of those with major depression had not received any mental health treatment (Nguyen *et al.* 2018).

Triggers

In ChildLine counselling sessions in 2013–14, young people with depression discussed how their depression had been triggered by life events, which included school pressures, bullying, abuse, bereavement and relationship difficulties (NSPCC 2014a). And the reasons given for feeling sad or down by girls aged 7 to 10 years in the 2015 Girl Guides Girls' Attitudes Survey were friendship problems, family problems, people at school and school work (Girl Guides Association 2015). The depression experienced by young people in the American study by Breslau *et al.* (2017) was also associated with problems with school and relationships. And in a 2004 study of teenagers aged 13 to 16 years in Ireland who had since recovered from their depression, family problems and bullying were the most common triggers reported (Fitzpatrick *et al.* 2004). The latest Good Childhood Report (Children's Society 2018) also found that 25% of children are subjected to comments and jokes about appearance on a non-stop basis, and that this has a negative effect on their life satisfaction and mental health.

Symptoms

In the same Irish study, the young people used words like 'sad', 'lonely', 'confused' and 'angry' to describe how they felt when depressed, and they also discussed symptoms of hopelessness, isolation, lack of confidence, loss of interest in things, difficulties concentrating, risk-taking and substance misuse (Fitzpatrick *et al.* 2004). A survey of over 5000 young people in schools (Action for Children 2018) found that 33% were struggling, with the most common problems being feeling depressed, difficulty sleeping,

The Depression Gazette Page 5

inability to shake negative feelings, struggling to 'get going', problems focusing, and feeling like everything is 'an effort'.

In ChildLine counselling sessions in 2013–14, young people with depression reported finding it hard to get out of bed in the morning and to face the day ahead (NSPCC 2014a). Some young people talked about suffering in silence as they didn't think they would be taken seriously and about feeling unable to cope, self-harming or feeling suicidal (NSPCC 2014a).

In 2010–11, ChildLine provided 8835 counselling sessions to young people who were thinking about or planning suicide. By 2015–16 this had increased to 19,841 counselling sessions (NSPCC 2016), and by 2016–17 this had reached 22,456 counselling sessions – the highest levels they had ever been (NSPCC 2017).

In 2016–17, 72% of these sessions were with girls (NSPCC 2017), yet statistics show that more males than females commit suicide (Office for National Statistics 2017). Suicide is the most common cause of death for boys aged 5 to 19 years, and the second most common for girls of this age in the UK (Wolfe *et al.* 2014). One hundred and forty-nine young people aged 10 to 19 years in England committed suicide in 2014 (Korkodilos 2016). Worldwide, suicide is the third leading cause of death among adolescents (World Health Organization 2001).

Many young people experiencing suicidal thoughts report feeling unable to tell anyone (NSPCC 2014b) because of a fear that 'other people won't understand what they are going through', or a worry about 'being judged', 'told off' or 'not taken seriously by their parents' (NSPCC 2017, p.38).

The national Adult Psychiatric Morbidity Survey in 2007 found that approximately 6% of 16- to 24-year-olds had attempted suicide and approximately 9% had self-harmed (McManus *et al.* 2009).

From 2001 to 2011, the number of young people admitted to hospital because of self-harm increased by 68% (YoungMinds 2011). In 2006, the Mental Health Foundation stated that between 1 in 12 and 1 in 15 children and young people self-harm. In 2016, Public Health England stated that this was now as high as 1 in 10. The Good Childhood Report (Children's Society 2018) found that 60% of children with high depressive symptoms had self-harmed.

The Depression Gazette Page 6

Gender, Gender Identity and Sexuality and Their Impact on Depression

The UK Household Longitudinal Survey in 2014–15 found that more females than males had symptoms of anxiety and depression (25% and 15% respectively) (Office for National Statistics 2017). This same gender difference was also found in a study by Patalay and Fitzsimons (2017) where 24% of all girls aged 14 years suffered from depression compared to only 9% of boys the same age. This equates to approximately 166,000 girls and 67,000 boys nationally (Patalay and Fitzsimons 2017). The 2018 Good Childhood Report (Children's Society 2018) also found that girls had lower life satisfaction than boys and that they were more likely to experience depressive symptoms (16.2%) than boys (5.8%).

There are several other studies that also highlight how girls are more likely to experience depression than boys (e.g. Collishaw 2015; Lessof *et al.* 2016; Public Health England 2016; World Health Organization 2017).

In 2014, the annual Girl Guides Girls' Attitudes Survey found that 73% of girls aged 11 to 21 years knew girls their age who were depressed (Girl Guides Association 2014). In 2015 the survey found that 83% of 7- to 10-year-old girls felt sad or down at least sometimes, with 7% feeling sad or down on most days and 3% feeling that way all the time (Girl Guides Association 2015). In 2016 the same survey found that 16% of girls aged 7 to 21 years were not happy and 69% felt like they weren't good enough (Girl Guides Association 2016).

Numerous studies are finding that girls are more likely to self-harm than boys (e.g. Brooks *et al.* 2015). The 2018 Good Childhood Report (Children's Society 2018) also found that girls are twice as likely (22%) as boys (9%) to self-harm.

The same report also found that 38% of gay, lesbian or bisexual young people experienced depressive symptoms and 46% had self-harmed. Stonewall's School Report (Guasp 2012) found that 49% of lesbian and bisexual girls and 29% of gay and bisexual boys had symptoms consistent with depression.

The same report also highlighted how 71% of lesbian and bisexual girls and 57% of gay and bisexual boys had experienced suicidal thoughts; 29% of lesbian and bisexual girls and 17% of gay and bisexual boys had made a suicide attempt; and 72% of lesbian and bisexual girls and 36% of gay and bisexual boys had self-harmed (Guasp 2012). A study by the charity MQ (2014) also found that over half of LGBT youth reported self-harm and almost half had considered suicide. LGBT young people who have experienced homophobic bullying are more likely to self-harm, have suicidal thoughts or make suicide attempts, and Guasp (2012) found that 41% of LGBT pupils who had experienced homophobic bullying said that was what had triggered their self-harm.

A survey by Nodin *et al.* (2014) found that 48% of transgender people under 26 years of age had attempted suicide, 59% had considered doing so, and 59% had self-harmed. A national online survey in Australia also found that 75% of young transgender people had been diagnosed with depression, 79% had self-harmed and 48% had attempted suicide (Strauss *et al.* 2017).

Treatment and Recovery

What works?

In an Irish study (Fitzpatrick *et al.* 2004), three-quarters of young people had found telling someone about how they were feeling and doing things to distract themselves helpful. Many also reported that stopping avoidance was beneficial. Two-thirds had obtained professional support, and the majority had found it helpful.

One form of professional support available is CBT. Many studies show CBT to be effective in the treatment of depression, and it is a recommended form of therapy for depression. Studies have also found CBT-based self-help to be effective (Gellatly *et al.* 2007; Williams *et al.* 2013).

Recovery

Studies show that most people with depression will recover – with 10% recovering after 3 months, 40% within the first year, and only 20% remaining depressed after 2 years (Goodyer, Herbert and Tamplin 2003; Harrington and Dubicka 2001).

Social Media and Depression

According to research, young people who spend more than 2 hours per day on social networking sites are more likely to experience mental health issues, including anxiety, depression and suicidal thoughts (Sampasa-Kanyinga and Lewis 2015).

The Depression Gazette Page 8

In particular, there are studies showing that increased or problematic use is associated with significantly increased levels of depression (Augner and Hacker 2012; Lin *et al.* 2016) – something researchers are now terming 'Facebook depression' (American Academy of Pediatrics 2017).

One of the main reasons suggested for this is that young people negatively compare themselves and their lives to those of others they see on social media sites, including comparing themselves to images that have been digitally manipulated and videos that have been staged. This can lead to a fear of missing out or inadequacy or a need to be constantly connected to others online because of a fear of missing out – a phenomenon now known as FOMO (Royal Society for Public Health 2017). FOMO has been found to be linked to lower mood and lower life satisfaction (Pryzbylski *et al.* 2013).

The national survey of children and young people's health in England (Sadler *et al.* 2018) also found that over half of all girls up to 19 years of age experiencing a mental health disorder reported comparing themselves to others on social media sites.

Thus, many are arguing that 'the intensity of the online world – where teens and young adults are constantly contactable, face pressures from unrealistic representations of reality, and deal with online peer pressure – may be responsible for triggering depression or exacerbating existing conditions' (Royal Society for Public Health 2017, p.8).

However, it is important to state that social media can also bring positive benefits for young people, including the ability to connect with others and gain support and advice from others in a way that they may not otherwise feel able to do or have access to in everyday life.

The Depression Gazette Page 9

YOUR VOICE! (PART 1)

If you could have your say on what is needed to address depression amongst young people today, what would you tell the politicians? Write a letter to your government with your suggestions in the space below. You can also produce a copy of this letter and send it to your local politician.

Tell the Government what you think!

Now take a look at the following pictures, poems and songs by other young people where they describe what depression is like for them.

Dark Cloud

I can't breathe
I'm suffocating under this blanket of sadness
Every moment
Of every day
There is a dark cloud over my head

I can't stop crying
I am so full of misery
Every moment
Of every day
There is a dark cloud over my head

I can't have fun
I am so empty
Every moment
Of every day
There is a dark cloud over my head

And with each passing moment
The dark cloud has taken away my hope, my dreams
Little by little
Piece by piece
Now the only way I can see the world is through my dark cloud.

By Tori, aged 16 years

By Viktor, aged 10 years

In My Room

My room is safe.
My bed is safer.
I can hide under the covers,
And pretend the rest of the world doesn't exist,
Because I can't face the world.
I can't cope in it.
I'm too tired to cope.
I feel useless and worthless.
I can't think,
And I can't eat.
I'm hopeless.
I'm a waste of space.
I'm ashamed of me.
What's the point of me?
What's the point of my life?
Life outside my room is too much.
Please just let me hide in here
In my room.

By Joel, aged 14 years

By Henrik, aged 13 years

Where Did All the Happiness Go?

I am so low
I'm sinking towards the centre of the Earth.
I am so upset
I'm in a puddle of tears.
I'm so empty
My soul has left.
I'm so tired
But I can't sleep.

The weight on my shoulders is so heavy
I can't move.
I'm so pathetic and helpless
I can't let others see me.
I want to feel happiness and excitement
But I've lost that part of me
And I don't know how to find it again.

By Nisha, aged 15 years

By Verity, aged 15 years

Depression and Me

Down
Empty
Pained
Rejected
Exhausted
Sad
Suffering
Isolated
Overwhelmed
No-one

Angry
Nothing matters
Defeated

Miserable
Excluded.

By Lewis, aged 10 years

By Susie, aged 11 years

In the Depression Box on the next page, try showing what your depression is like through one of the following creative methods:

- draw a picture or take a photo or series of photos
- write a song, rap or poem
- write a short story or play
- write a blog
- draw or write down ideas for a short film
- draw or write down ideas for a dance piece.

DEPRESSION BOX

Let's get creative

STARVING THE DEPRESSION GREMLIN STEP 2

Treatments and Self-Help Strategies

Well done! You have completed Step 1 towards starving your Depression Gremlin – learning about depression in general and your own personal experience of it. Now, for Step 2 – learning about different types of treatments and self-help strategies that can help you to starve your Depression Gremlin and applying those that will work best for you to help get your depression under control.

So, the chapters that follow will look at:

- the different types of treatment available for depression
- self-help strategies for depression, including thinking and acting differently
- specific things you can do if you are feeling suicidal.

9

Speaking to a Professional about Types of Treatment

Speaking to a Professional

If you feel comfortable doing so, it can be extremely beneficial to speak to a healthcare practitioner, such as your GP, or a mental health practitioner, such as a psychologist, psychiatrist, counsellor or therapist, about how you are feeling. Doing so can help you to starve your Depression Gremlin. It is a vital thing to do if you are experiencing severe depression or if your depression is accompanied by other mental health disorders, such as an eating disorder, or negative coping strategies like substance abuse or self-harming. Don't worry, as these professionals talk to people about depression every day.

Before you go, write down your symptoms, how long you have had them for and the impacts they are having on you, and take this with you. Also, write down any questions you might have, for example about types of treatment. This will help you feel more comfortable.

GPs and mental health practitioners can help you to starve your Depression Gremlin by:

- providing you with a diagnosis
- discussing the best treatment options for you
- looking at whether medication is appropriate
- referring you to the people and services that can help or provide them directly.

Speaking to a professional about how you are feeling also enables them to check in with you regularly to ensure your depression is reducing and to recommend other forms of treatment if needed.

So, what types of treatment exist that can help you to starve your Depression Gremlin and overcome your depression?

Types of Treatment: Self-Help Versions

ACTIVE MONITORING/WATCHFUL WAITING

If your depression is mild, in the first instance your GP is likely to just monitor you for a couple of weeks to see if your depression improves by itself. This is what GPs call...

'active monitoring' or 'watchful waiting'.

BIBLIOTHERAPY

For some young people, if their depression is mild, working through a...

self-help book

...like *Starving the Depression Gremlin* may be the most appropriate way forward and may be all that is needed to get their depression under control. We call this...

bibliotherapy.

And this is what you are doing right now!

Your GP can provide you with a prescription for certain self-help books that you can loan for free from your local library under the Reading Well for Young People Books on Prescription service, or you can ask for them yourself at your library.[1]

GUIDED SELF-HELP

This is where a professional works through self-help books with you, usually over a period of six to eight sessions. This can sometimes be provided by a Psychological Wellbeing Practitioner (PWP) within your GP practice, by a Learning Mentor or Pastoral Care within your

1 For a full list of books currently available see http://reading-well.org.uk/books/books-on-prescription/young-people-mental-health.

school or via another organisation, such as a Multi-Agency Support Team (MAST), who can be asked to work with you and your family where appropriate.

COMPUTERISED CBT

As we learned in Chapter 1 of this workbook, CBT is where a therapist helps people to deal with a wide range of emotional problems, including depression, by looking at the links between our cognition, physical reactions, emotions and behaviours and how we can change how we feel by changing how we think and act. Computerised CBT is another form of self-help and it teaches you CBT-based techniques for managing your depression using computer software packages, apps or via websites.

Types of Treatment: Talking Therapies

Sometimes, self-help tools alone are not enough to help a person suffering from depression make all the progress that they need to, for example:

- when an individual is experiencing moderate to severe depression
- where their depression is accompanied by other mental health disorders, such as an eating disorder
- where their depression is accompanied by negative coping strategies like substance abuse or self-harming.

In such cases, a form of talking therapy is likely to be recommended, but this workbook is still suitable to be used alongside professional support.

Within the UK, an organisation called the National Institute for Health and Care Excellence (NICE) looks at the evidence on how effective different forms of treatment are for a variety of different health and mental health conditions and makes recommendations about which treatments should be used. For children and young people with depression, NICE (2005) recommends individual or group CBT, interpersonal psychotherapy (IPT), family therapy or psychodynamic psychotherapy. Mindfulness-based cognitive therapy (MBCT) and behavioural activation are two other forms of therapy for depression that NICE (2009) recommends for adults. However, there is a growing body of research highlighting their effectiveness for children and young people too. Person-centred counselling can also be used for depression, but there isn't as much research available on its effectiveness.

Let's look at each of these in turn.

INDIVIDUAL OR GROUP CBT

Individual CBT is a brief form of therapy – often lasting no more than 12 to 16 sessions – which is recommended and proven to be effective for depression and is provided by a professional trained to deliver CBT, such as a CBT therapist or psychologist. During the sessions you will learn about what depression is, how it develops, its symptoms and how it is affecting you. You will also receive help to identify negative patterns of thoughts and behaviours and learn how to change these in order to manage your depression.

In group CBT, you will learn about depression and how to use CBT techniques to improve depression along with other people who are also experiencing depression instead of on your own. It gives you the opportunity to talk to and gain support from others with similar experiences and to realise that you are not on your own in how you are feeling.

IPT

IPT is another recommended form of brief therapy for depression. It is based on the idea that depression can occur when difficulties arise in our important relationships and helps people to identify the relationship problems they are experiencing and to find ways to tackle them. The number of professionals providing IPT in the UK is still limited, however, so you may find it difficult to access this form of therapy. But you may be able to tackle these same issues as part of CBT or family therapy.

FAMILY THERAPY

Through family therapy, family members can share their thoughts and feelings with each other, gain a better understanding of the experiences and needs of each other, and find ways to deal with any relationship difficulties between them that may be having negative impacts on them, their health and mental health, and their lives.

PSYCHODYNAMIC PSYCHOTHERAPY

Psychodynamic psychotherapy focuses on how our past experiences and relationships, especially in childhood, may be having an impact upon how we are feeling in the present. This can often be a long-term therapy.

MBCT

MBCT is also a recommended form of therapy that is proving to be effective for depression. It teaches us to:

- focus on the present and appreciate the positive things around us, without dwelling on the past or worrying about the future
- see thoughts as merely thoughts and let them go in a non-judgemental way
- choose how to act in situations instead of reacting on 'autopilot'
- calm our minds and bodies using breathing, meditation and relaxation.

BEHAVIOURAL ACTIVATION

Behavioural activation is a form of therapy for depression that can form part of CBT or can be offered on its own. It is based on the idea that what we do affects how we feel. It suggests that by doing more things that we enjoy, value and gain a sense of achievement from, and by reducing how much we act in negative ways, we can help to improve our mood.

PERSON-CENTRED COUNSELLING

Person-centred counselling involves expressing how you feel to a trained counsellor who will listen to you, empathise with you and support you to find your own ways forward in a non-judgemental way, but without giving advice.

HOW TO ACCESS TALKING THERAPIES

In the UK, some forms of talking treatments can be accessed for free on the NHS via a referral from your GP to an appropriate mental health practitioner – either within your GP practice itself or within the Child and Adolescent Mental Health Service (CAMHS). Some schools also provide a within-school counselling service for their pupils, and schools can also refer pupils to CAMHS. You can also access support through other counselling services that may be available in your area, either provided by charities or by mental health practitioners in private practice, or obtain phone or online support via organisations, such as ChildLine and the Samaritans. Please see Appendices 1 and 2 for information on some of the support options available.

Types of Treatment: Other Therapies

Other therapies can also be used for depression, including:

- *Art, music and drama therapies* – these can enable people who are having difficulty talking about their feelings to express them and address them in a more creative way. Your GP, mental health practitioner or school may be able to recommend practitioners in your area.

- *Light therapy* – this is a form of therapy specifically for people whose depression is seasonal and caused by changes in natural light levels from season to season. There are a number of studies that have found light therapy to be beneficial for young people with Seasonal Affective Disorder (e.g. Walter and Ghaziuddin 2009). It involves sitting near a light box emitting artificial light that mimics natural outdoor light for periods of time in the autumn and winter. Please discuss this with your GP first.

- *Complementary therapies* – these can include acupuncture, homeopathy, massage and herbal medicine, and they focus on healing the body as a whole. Some people find them to be effective for their depression. If you are considering herbal medicine, please ensure that you discuss this with your GP first if you are taking any pharmaceutical medications,

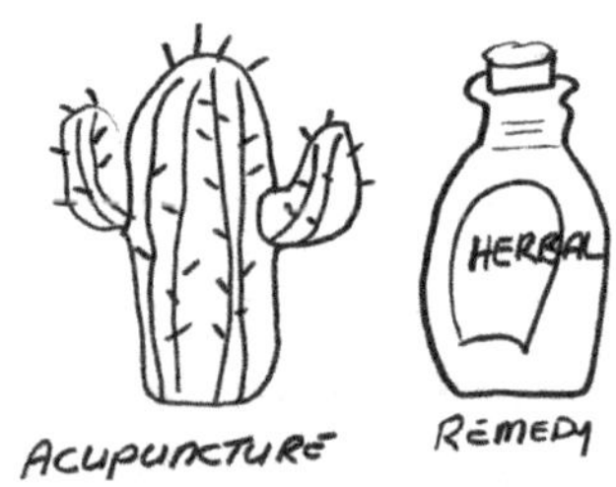

and also be aware that one form of herbal medicine used for depression, St John's Wort, is not recommended for children and young people.

Types of Treatment: Antidepressant Medication

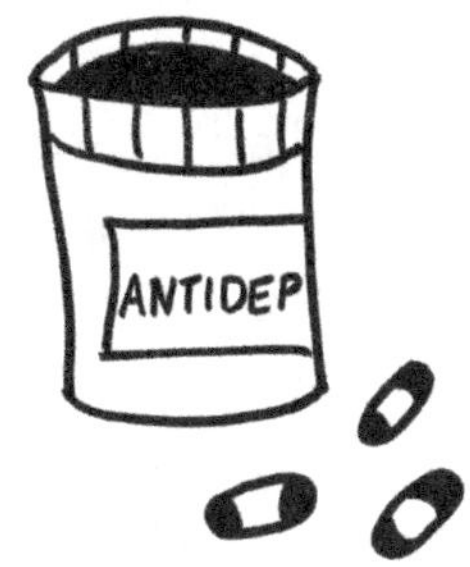

According to guidelines issued by NICE, antidepressant medications should:

- only be prescribed to children and young people in exceptional circumstances, especially for children under 12 years of age where their effectiveness has not been established
- only be used for cases of moderate to severe depression
- be accompanied by therapy unless it is refused.

There are many different types of antidepressant medications, but the one that is recommended for young people is Fluoxetine (also known by the brand name Prozac), as it is the only one where studies have shown the benefits to outweigh the risk of negative side-effects for young people. The usual starting dose is 10mg.

It can take up to six weeks for people to start feeling any effects from antidepressants. A GP or psychiatrist will usually continue to prescribe the antidepressant for approximately six months after the person feels improved and then phase them out over a period of 6 to 12 weeks. However, the length of time a person needs to be taking them for will depend on how severe their depression is and how effective the medication is for them. You must follow the exact instructions on how and when to take them and you will need regular check-ups from your GP whilst taking them. It is also important for a young person to be closely monitored by a psychiatrist whilst taking antidepressants.

Not every antidepressant will work for everyone, and some people will experience negative side-effects, such as headaches, nausea, drowsiness, diarrhoea or constipation, loss of appetite, dry mouth, dizziness, blurred vision, excessive sweating, shakiness, agitation, nervousness, sleep problems or an initial worsening of their existing symptoms of depression. Young people may also become irritable or over-excited. However, in general, the side-effects are mild and short-lived.

But, if you are prescribed Fluoxetine and you find it has had no impact on how you are feeling or if you experience negative side-effects that are too severe or that don't subside quickly, it is important to speak to your GP, as your antidepressant dosage may need changing or you may need to be prescribed an alternative antidepressant, such as Sertraline or Citalopram. Speak to your GP or psychiatrist immediately if you get a rash, feel more aggressive, feel suicidal for the first time or have increased suicidal thoughts after taking antidepressants. Some people may also experience something called 'mania' when they take antidepressants. This can involve suddenly becoming extremely overactive or irritable, feeling 'wired' or acting in unusually risky ways. Please speak to your GP or psychiatrist straight away if this happens. Do not just suddenly stop taking the antidepressants yourself, as withdrawal symptoms can occur.

Antidepressants work on brain chemicals, such as serotonin, which can help to treat the symptoms of depression and lift a person's mood. However, they are not 'happy pills'! When they work for a person, they will give a 'chemical boost' to bring his or her mood up to a level where he or she is more able to cope and to start implementing strategies to tackle the causes of his or her depression.[2]

2 For more information on medications used for mental health issues, visit the excellent HeadMeds website run by the mental health charity YoungMinds at www.headmeds.org.uk.

Types of Treatment: Other Medical Treatments

If you are experiencing a 'depressive disorder due to another medical condition', then treatments designed to improve your medical condition may also have a knock-on effect of improving your mood, such as B12 injections for B12 deficiency or physiotherapy for an injury that is triggering depression. If you have depression as a side-effect of a prescribed medication, you are likely to be prescribed an alternative medication, and if you are experiencing Premenstrual Dysphoric Disorder, you may be prescribed medications to improve the balance of your hormones, such as oestrogen and progesterone.

So, now that you have learned about a variety of treatments for depression, let's look at changes you can make yourself as part of your continued self-help or bibliotherapy.

10

An Introduction to Self-Help Strategies

Thomas Jefferson, an 18th-century American politician who drafted the country's declaration of independence, said:

> *'If you want something you've never had, you must be willing to do something you've never done.'*

And Albert Einstein said:

> *'If you always do what you always did, you will always get what you always got.'*

These wise words mean that if we want things about ourselves and our lives to change, we need to do something different. So, if we want our depression to change, we need to...

THINK DIFFERENTLY	and	ACT DIFFERENTLY

...because, no matter what has triggered your depression, it's your thoughts and behaviours that are feeding your Depression Gremlin, making him grow bigger and bigger and keeping you stuck in the vicious cycle of depression!

We ***can't*** change the difficult life experiences and interactions with others that we have experienced in the past, and we may not have control over certain life experiences and interactions in the present or future, but what we ***can*** change is how we think about them and ourselves and how we act in response to them.

When we are depressed, making such changes can seem impossible because we are lacking in motivation and energy, feeling hopeless and thinking negatively. But, if we set ourselves realistic goals for change, take small steps towards these goals and be proud of each achievement along the way, then changing how we think and act ***is*** possible. And your Depression Gremlin will get smaller...

...and your depression will improve!

It can be harder for people to keep their thoughts in perspective if they:

- have experienced depression before
- have been exposed to other people responding to life situations in depressed ways
- are experiencing or have experienced other emotional or mental health issues, such as anxiety or low self-esteem.

These all have the potential to make us ***more susceptible*** to:

- thinking, feeling and acting in negative ways
- feeding our Depression Gremlin
- experiencing depression.

However, they do not ***cause*** us to have depression, they just make us ***more susceptible*** to experiencing it. But we don't have to. We have a choice as to how we respond to situations.

When our depression has a biological trigger, such as our body's reaction to a medical condition, medications, substances, hormones or seasons (as you learnt in Chapter 4 of this workbook), we can also find it much harder to keep our thoughts in perspective and to act in constructive ways. However, again, we can learn strategies to help improve the way we think and act in order to improve our mood.

So, let's start by thinking differently!

11

Thinking Differently!

Do you remember that it is how you think about life experiences and interactions with others that can trigger and/or worsen your depression? Do you remember that if you are wearing a pair of Depression Thinking Glasses you are feeding your Depression Gremlin? To stop this and to starve your Depression Gremlin, you need to learn how to...

think differently!

And that is what this chapter is all about! By doing so, you will feel calmer, more positive and more able to cope in life, and your depression will reduce.

The methods of thinking differently that we will look at are:

- accepting that you have depression
- accepting that thoughts are only thoughts
- not fearing feelings
- being in the moment
- ditching your Depression Thinking Glasses using realistic thinking
- making realistic thinking easier
- thought-testing experiments
- dealing with memories
- using visualisation
- using techniques to help improve cognitive skills.

So, let's start with the first way in which you can think differently.

Accepting that You Have Depression

People experiencing depression can spend so much time:

- beating themselves up for being depressed
- asking, 'Why did this have to happen to me?'
- telling themselves they are a failure or useless because they have depression
- focusing on the unfairness of the situation, or even
- denying that their depression exists.

But, this way of thinking only feeds your Depression Gremlin and keeps you trapped in the cycle of depression.

So, a key way in which you can think differently is to accept that you have depression and that having it doesn't make you a failure. Acceptance is key to being able to move forward.

Accepting that Thoughts Are Only Thoughts

In Chapter 1 of this workbook, I told you a little bit about something called mindfulness. Mindfulness can help us to starve our Depression Gremlin by teaching us to:

- become AWARE of our thoughts in the here and now without being overwhelmed by them, eaten up by them or reacting to them in a negative way
- ACCEPT that our thoughts are only thoughts and that they cannot hurt us unless we let them
- LET our thoughts GO, just like leaves blowing away in the wind.

Why not try an exercise to help you practise letting go of your thoughts? Get a piece of paper and on it write a negative thought that you have about yourself or your life or the people or world around you that is feeding your Depression Gremlin. Then say out loud, 'This is only a thought and it cannot hurt me.' Next, scrunch up the piece of paper and throw it in the bin, and as you do, imagine your thought blowing away in the wind, just like those leaves! And visualise your Depression Gremlin shrinking!

Not Fearing Feelings

When we are depressed, it can feel easier to avoid feelings, as they can seem scary, distressing, uncontrollable things. But, if you acknowledge they exist, tell yourself it is OK for them to exist and then let them go or address them in another constructive way, they will no longer be a thing to fear or avoid.

Being in the Moment

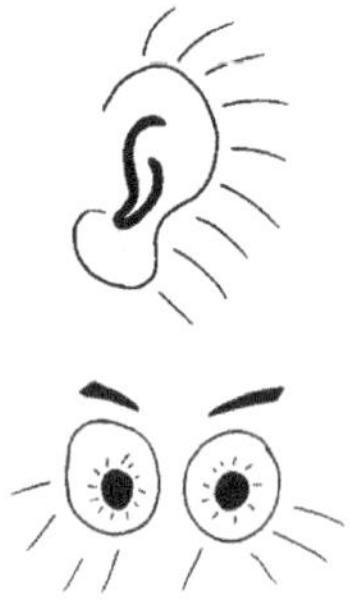

Mindfulness teaches us the importance of being in the moment, without being distracted by negative thinking about the past or the future. Focus your attention on the detail of what you're doing, your surroundings, and any sights, smells, sounds and tastes – use all your senses! Appreciate the positives in the present moment and pay real attention to them. By paying attention to the here and now in this way, you are less likely to get stuck in your negative thoughts – thereby living fully in the world around you.

Ditching Your Depression Thinking Glasses Using Realistic Thinking

Earlier in this workbook we learnt about different types of Depression Thinking Glasses. And remember, the more we wear our Depression Thinking Glasses by thinking in negative and unrealistic ways about ourselves, our lives and life events, our future and the world and other people around us, the more we feed our Depression Gremlin and the more depressed we feel. So how do we ditch our Depression Thinking Glasses and starve our Depression Gremlin? First, by...

catching our thoughts

...which means noticing the ones that are potentially negative and unrealistic. And second, by challenging them using something called...

realistic thinking.

Realistic thinking involves searching for facts, just like a detective searching for evidence. To search for facts, ask yourself questions like those on the next page.

What am I thinking?

Is this thought helpful right now?

What are the facts about the situation?

Is my thought based on the facts?

Do I have any evidence to back up my thought?

What are the advantages and disadvantages of my thought?

Am I thinking factually about the present or am I imagining the future or obsessing over the past?

Which pair of Depression Thinking Glasses am I wearing?

What effects will this way of thinking have on my body, emotions and behaviours?

What is the worst thing that could happen and is it really that likely?

What is more likely to happen?

If the worst thing happened, would it really be that bad or would I cope somehow?

What would I tell a friend in the same situation as me?

What is a more realistic way of thinking about the situation based on the facts?

What will be the effects of thinking a more realistic thought?

As you get more and more practised at thinking differently by searching for the facts, you should find yourself:

- wearing your Depression Thinking Glasses less and less
- starving your Depression Gremlin more and more
- feeling less and less depressed.

And your Depression Gremlin should shrink more and more!

So, whenever you find yourself putting on your Depression Thinking Glasses, take them off and start to ***think more realistically*** about yourself, your life and life events, your future and other people and the world around you ***based on the facts***.

Make sure you aren't being overly negative in some way or blowing things out of proportion. Remember, situations are normally not as bad as we think they are going to be, and even if our worst-case scenario actually occurs, we can find a way to cope with it, learn from it and move on from it. Also, non-stop negative thinking about the past won't help us. We can't change the past, just how we think about it, and whether we are going to let it take over our present and negatively affect our future or not.

Realistic thinking isn't easy to do and can take some practice, but it is well worth trying! Some people find thinking of a red traffic light or a stop sign when they have a negative or unrealistic thought helps them to break out of that thought ready to challenge it. This is called...

thought stopping.

Let's look at an example to give you some practice at thinking realistically.

CADEN'S STORY

Caden is 15 years old. His mum and dad were always fighting, and when Caden was 12 years old, his dad had an affair and divorced Caden's mum. He hasn't seen his dad since. His mum didn't know how to cope with what had happened and she began drinking alcohol excessively. She now spends most of her time drinking or sleeping.

Since his mum developed a problem with alcohol, Caden has done all the shopping, made all his own meals, cleaned the house and washed all his own clothes. And even with all this on his plate, Caden still did really well at school.

Last year, a new boy called Luke started at Caden's school and they became really good friends. Caden started to spend lots of time at Luke's house, which included having meals with Luke's family, getting help with his homework from Luke's parents and sleeping over most weekends. At first, Caden was so happy, but after a while, the more time he spent with Luke's family, the sadder he felt.

Caden couldn't stop thinking, 'I must be a really bad person as I don't have a family like Luke's'; 'My dad must have left us as I wasn't a perfect son like Luke'; and 'If I was a better person, my mum would love me like Luke's mum loves him.' Eventually, he stopped going to Luke's house and his school grades dropped as he kept thinking, 'What's the point of studying? No-one cares whether I do well or not.'

His teachers have tried to speak to him to find out what is wrong, but he just gets angry with them. Luke tried to speak to him at school, but Caden kept ignoring him, so Luke has started to make other friends. Caden can't stop thinking, 'Luke probably never really liked me anyway. I was just a stop gap until he found better friends.'

Caden barely eats now and goes days without washing himself. He spends his evenings and weekends in bed as he feels exhausted all the time and doesn't enjoy doing anything else any more. He has also started skipping school, instead spending his time drinking his mum's alcohol and thinking, 'What is the point of my life? I would be better off dead. No-one would miss me. No-one is ever going to care for me or love me.'

Q. Are Caden's thoughts based on facts? Tick your answer.

YES ☐ NO ☐

Q. Is Caden wearing Depression Thinking Glasses? Tick your answer.

YES ☐ NO ☐

Q. If your answer was 'Yes', which ones do you think he is wearing?

....

....

....

....

....

Q. Which thoughts could Caden accept as only thoughts and which thoughts could he let go of or challenge based on facts?

....

....

....

....

....

Q. What realistic thoughts could Caden have instead?

....

....

....

....

....

If you said that Caden's thoughts aren't based on facts, you are correct. Caden is wearing several different types of Depression Thinking Glasses, such as:

- Magnifying Glasses

- Make Believe Glasses
- Fortune Telling Glasses
- Mind Reading Glasses
- Doom and Gloom Glasses
- I'm Useless Glasses
- I Should Glasses
- Self-blame Glasses
- What's the Point Glasses
- Ignoring the Good Glasses.

Caden needs to let go of his negative thoughts about himself, his life, his future and other people and the world around him and think more realistically, such as:

FACT 1

Caden's dad leaving wasn't his fault.

FACT 2

There are people in Caden's life that care about him.

Some people find it easier to challenge their thoughts by saying them out loud or to other people. Others find writing the process down more helpful, especially in the initial stages. This allows you to use these notes again in the future if you have similar thoughts.

At first, you might struggle with catching and challenging the thought as it happens. Don't worry about this. Just start by challenging any thoughts you need to after they have occurred. If you find it hard to remember your thoughts, try playing back what happened visually in your mind like watching a film, as this can help some people to remember.

The Alternative Thoughts Worksheet that follows will help you with challenging your thoughts. It will help you to ditch your Depression Thinking Glasses, think more realistically and starve your Depression Gremlin! Try using it when you need to challenge negative and unrealistic thoughts about yourself, your life and life events, your future, other people and the world around you. Once you get used to this, it will become easier to catch and challenge your thoughts as they occur in the here and now.

Alternative Thoughts Worksheet

Write or draw your answers to the questions in the spaces below.

What is the situation?

What am I thinking?

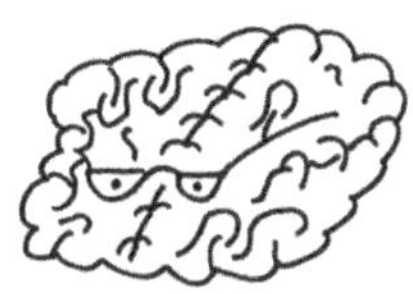

Am I thinking through any of the following Depression Thinking Glasses? (Colour in or tick any that apply to your thoughts.)

MAGNIFYING	MAKE BELIEVE	FORTUNE TELLING
ALL OR NOTHING	WHAT IF?	MIND READING
DOOM AND GLOOM	MY FEELINGS ARE FACTS	SELF-BLAME
UNHAPPY MEMORIES	I SHOULD	WHAT'S THE POINT?
IGNORING THE GOOD	I CAN'T	I'M USELESS

What facts and evidence do I need to be aware of?

Are my thoughts based on these facts or evidence? Tick which answer applies to you.

YES ☐ NO ☐

Are my thoughts feeding or starving my Depression Gremlin? Tick which answer applies to you.

FEEDING ☐ STARVING ☐

How can I think more realistically based on the facts and evidence in order to starve my Depression Gremlin?

Making Realistic Thinking Easier

Here are some things to remember when challenging your negative and unrealistic thoughts and beliefs about yourself, your life and life events, your future, other people and the world around you in order to make realistic thinking easier:

- We are all worthy and equal.
- Perfection doesn't exist.
- Mistakes and weaknesses do not equal failure.
- We don't know what other people are thinking.
- Other people's opinions are not facts.
- We can't please everyone all of the time.
- The past doesn't have to equal the present or the future.
- There will be positives in your life.
- It's OK to be different.
- Being true to our 'real' selves is important.
- Knowing our values is important.
- Seeing the bigger picture of ourselves is important.

WE ARE ALL WORTHY AND EQUAL

Many people with depression have low self-confidence or self-esteem and see themselves as unworthy or not as worthy as other people. However, everyone who exists on this planet is worthy and equal.

PERFECTION DOESN'T EXIST

When we are depressed, we can often place expectations on ourselves that are unrealistic or that place too much pressure on us, such as 'I need to be perfect'. And we can sometimes believe that we need to live up to unrealistic expectations like perfection in order to please other people or to make them like us or to try to fit in. But we would never achieve such an expectation because no-one is good at everything. Perfection doesn't exist!

So, in order to starve your Depression Gremlin, remind yourself that you can only ever do your best and achieve things that are ***realistic for you*** based on your strengths, abilities and current circumstances. And remember, ***perfection doesn't exist***!

As a famous quote by Albert Einstein says:

'Everybody is a genius. But if you judge a fish by its ability to climb a tree, it will live its whole life believing that it is stupid.'

In the next Depression Box, list any expectations that you place on yourself that you now realise are unrealistic and then write down more realistic expectations for yourself.

DEPRESSION BOX

MY UNREALISTIC EXPECTATIONS	ALTERNATIVE REALISTIC EXPECTATIONS

MISTAKES AND WEAKNESSES DO NOT EQUAL FAILURE

We all make mistakes and we all have weaknesses. They are a normal part of being human. We must learn to accept that making them and having them does not make us a failure. It just means we are human like everyone else! So, give yourself permission to make mistakes and forgive yourself when you make them – they are not the end of the world!

WE DON'T KNOW WHAT OTHER PEOPLE ARE THINKING

Unless you have mind-reading super powers, you actually have no idea what other people are thinking about you. And yet, we often worry about what other people think, and predict what they are thinking at times – we wear the 'mind-reading' Depression Thinking Glasses! And when we are depressed, we tend to think that other people are thinking negative things about us, such as we are 'ugly' or 'stupid'. But remember, we don't know what other people are thinking, and other people rarely judge you as harshly as you judge yourself. We are normally our own worst critics!

OTHER PEOPLE'S OPINIONS ARE NOT FACTS

It's important to remember that even if someone does think or say something negative about you, it doesn't make it fact! For example, perhaps you miss a penalty in a football final and one of your team mates calls you 'a useless loser'. It doesn't mean you are. That person has formed their own opinion about you, but that does not mean that they have objectively assessed your character based on fact. It is just their opinion. The fact is you missed a penalty, not that you are 'a useless loser'!

WE CAN'T PLEASE EVERYONE ALL OF THE TIME

You can't please all of the people all of the time because you're not responsible for how ***other people*** feel. You can only control how *you* feel. Not pleasing others doesn't make you a bad person. And focusing more on what you want from your life doesn't either! In fact, doing the latter will help you to learn more about the 'real' you and be confident in yourself and your abilities – thus starving your Depression Gremlin!

In the next Depression Box, list at least five things that you want to achieve in the next year because you want to and not because you think other people would approve of them!

DEPRESSION BOX

Things I want to achieve in the future

THE PAST DOESN'T HAVE TO EQUAL THE PRESENT OR THE FUTURE

Past events are merely indicators of what happened at that point in our lives, not predictors of the future. It is important to think factually about the present instead of worrying about the past or trying to predict the future using your Fortune Telling Depression Thinking Glasses!

And remember that you can't predict your whole future based on one specific event! So just because you may have failed one exam in the past, it doesn't mean you are going to fail every exam you take from here on in!

Also, if you spend so much time predicting negative things for your future, you don't notice the good things in the present day. So, when you find yourself predicting the future, turn your focus back to the present and the current positives in your life.

THERE WILL BE POSITIVES IN YOUR LIFE

I can hear you shouting, 'There are no positives!' because when we are depressed it is easy to feel like everything in life is going wrong and everything in life is rubbish. If you feel this way, it is important to think realistically about your life and look for the positives within it – I'm sure they will be there! Why not have a go at writing down the positives in your life in the Depression Box on the next page and regularly look at these when times feel tough.

DEPRESSION BOX

Positives in my life

Also, why not keep a list of positive things that happen in your life each day?

IT'S OK TO BE DIFFERENT

Q. What do you think it would be like to live on this planet if everyone was exactly the same?

. . . .

. . . .

. . . .

All of us are different and unique in many ways, and that is how it is meant to be. We are all supposed to have different talents, skills, abilities, characteristics, traits, looks, etc. If we didn't, how would we be able to fill all the jobs that are needed in society? Because of this, comparing ourselves to others is a waste of time. We aren't all meant to be the same. For example, intelligence doesn't come in one single form. It's not all about having a high IQ or being gifted at Maths and English. As humans we have 'multiple intelligences', which can include things such as practical intelligence and creative intelligence. So, your best friend may be great at languages, but it doesn't mean you have to be the same. Your best skill may be in ballet, martial arts or photography – and that is just as fantastic! Celebrate who you are and what you are good at – and don't ever feel that you aren't good enough! This will help you to starve your Depression Gremlin!

BEING TRUE TO OUR 'REAL' SELVES IS IMPORTANT

It is important to be true to your 'real' self and not to the kind of person others think you should be by:

- recognising the 'real' you
- accepting the 'real' you
- working on becoming the best version of the 'real' you that you can and that is realistic for you
- being proud of you!

KNOWING OUR VALUES IS IMPORTANT

Knowing your values will help you to be true to the 'real' you. Our values are things that we view as important in the way we live our lives. They are the things that we measure the success and happiness of our lives by. Many people today view their appearance or their wealth as more important than their health or their future goals or achievements. But this is leading to many of the negative impacts that we have seen in earlier chapters. Learning about our values can help us to respond in ways that reflect these values in situations and, as a result, be true to our 'real' selves. For example, Felix, a 15-year-old young person experiencing depression, described his values as:

- 'I see being a good friend as important.'
- 'I see being healthy as important.'
- 'I see being successful in my future career as important.'
- 'I see passing my exams as important.'
- 'I see being emotionally calm and happy as important.'

In the next Depression Box, list any values that are important to you. Make sure you are including values that are truly important to you, not just the ones you think other people will approve of.

DEPRESSION BOX

My values

SEEING THE BIGGER PICTURE OF OURSELVES IS IMPORTANT

You cannot define yourself solely on one perceived weakness. Yes, your weaknesses make up part of who you are, but so do all your positive characteristics, traits, talents, skills and abilities. And yes, we all have them, and you are no exception! You will have achieved many different things in your life that you can be proud of too!

It is therefore important to focus on the bigger picture about yourself instead of just on one or two specific aspects. It's not about looking at yourself through rose-tinted glasses for the sake of it. It's about looking at yourself positively based on what is factual and therefore realistic. Be a detective again, searching for the facts!

The following three activities will help you to do this. You may struggle to complete some of these activities at first if your confidence and self-esteem are low, but it is important to keep working on them, as they will help you to starve your Depression Gremlin, manage your depression and believe in yourself and your abilities!

In the next Depression Box, list at least ten positive things about yourself and write down a piece of evidence to back up each statement. These could be positive qualities and characteristics, things you are good at or your strengths, skills and talents. To give you an example, here are two things that Josie, aged 12 years, said about herself with accompanying evidence when learning how to overcome her own depression:

- 'I am a helpful person because I help my brother with his homework.'
- 'I am a kind person because I always give my friends hugs when they are feeling upset.'

DEPRESSION BOX

POSITIVES ABOUT ME	SUPPORTING EVIDENCE

Now list at least five things you have achieved in your life so far and write down at least one positive thing that each achievement shows you about yourself in the next Depression Box.

DEPRESSION BOX

MY ACHIEVEMENTS	POSITIVE THINGS THEY SHOW ABOUT ME

It can be helpful to keep a daily achievements diary in which you can record things you have achieved that day and what they show you about yourself.

Finally, based on everything you've come up with so far, write down five positive statements about yourself in the next Depression Box. We call these...

positive affirmations.

To help you with this, here are Josie's positive affirmations:

- 'I am a good sister.'
- 'I am a good friend.'

- 'I am a kind person.'
- 'I am a helpful person.'
- 'I am a caring person.'

DEPRESSION BOX

My positive affirmations

Remind yourself of these regularly. Say them out loud or put them somewhere you will see them every day. You can even send yourself a daily email or text with them written out!

Thinking about all the positive and realistic things about yourself in this way will help you to contradict your unrealistic and overly negative thoughts and to develop more positive and realistic ones – thereby helping to starve your Depression Gremlin!

Thought-Testing Experiments

Another helpful way of gathering evidence to help you challenge your thoughts is to become a scientist and do...

thought-testing experiments.

This is where you test out your thoughts through actions. Here is one young person's story as an example.

HATTIE'S DANCING EXPERIMENT

Hattie, aged 12 years, tested out the thought that she was no good at anything by joining a local street dance club. She was so afraid of going that she nearly backed out at the last minute. But she went in the end, and proved to herself that she was strong enough to do something new and that she was good at it – so good in fact that the club asked her to take part in their next stage performance.

You can use the following Thought-Testing Worksheet to help you design and complete your own experiments.

Thought-Testing Worksheet

Write or draw your answers to the questions in the spaces below.

Which thought do I want to test?

How will I test it?

What do I expect the result to be?

What was the result?

What have I learned from this result?

Did this thought feed or starve my Depression Gremlin?

FEED ☐ STARVE ☐

How can I make my thoughts more realistic and factual based on this result?

Dealing with Memories

When we are depressed, we can often focus on negative memories from our past. This can make us feel worse, especially if we use these memories to support our negative thinking. But, it is important to remember that our memories are not 100% accurate, factual video playbacks of what happened. Instead, we are directing the film that is playing back – adapting our memories based on thoughts and feelings at the time and our current mood and mindset.

So, in order to help starve your Depression Gremlin, you can:

- let these memories go
- look at them more realistically
- change them in some way to make them less powerful.

Using Visualisation

Another great way of thinking differently to help you starve your Depression Gremlin is to use something called...

visualisation.

This can involve picturing something in your head or thinking of memories that make you feel happy or relaxed or that make you laugh. Or you can picture yourself in a happy place. This can help you to feel calm at times when you are struggling or to help boost your mood when you are feeling low.

Another way in which you can use visualisation is to imagine things you want to achieve and picture yourself achieving them. This is a technique that sports people use to help motivate themselves mentally. For example, a runner might visualise themselves using the best possible running technique and winning their race in a personal best! You can also think about things in life that you are finding difficult or struggling to cope with and picture yourself tackling those difficulties and how, so you can feel prepared and more confident in your abilities.

You can also visualise your negative thoughts and feelings being put in the bin or floating away like those leaves we talked about earlier.

Or you can imagine that your negative and unrealistic thoughts are bubbles or balloons and that you are popping them!

Using Techniques to Help Improve Cognitive Skills

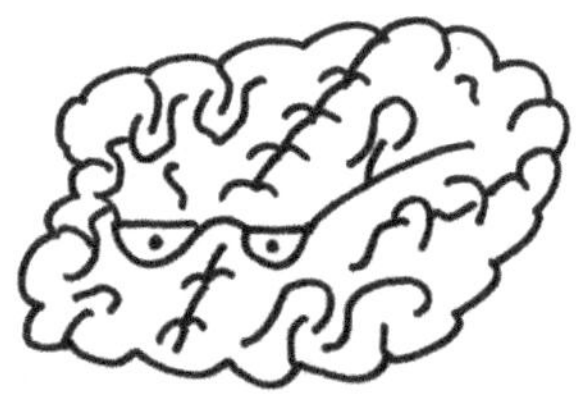

As we mentioned in Chapter 5, when we are depressed, our brains can struggle to function in several ways, including:

- Concentrating, focusing and paying attention
- Understanding information (we call this 'comprehension')
- Following processes or sequences, such as a recipe
- Gathering thoughts into a logical and clear format
- Putting thoughts down on paper or saying them out loud in a clear and reasoned way
- Remembering things
- Making decisions
- Reading

To help improve these cognitive skills, it is important to practise them. So, why not:

- try crosswords, craft activities, jigsaws, drawing or painting to help you practise concentrating
- follow a cookery recipe to practise following sequences
- search on the internet for fun memory games you can play.

When trying to improve your concentration, it can also help to start by concentrating for only a very short period and then gradually keep increasing the length of time you concentrate on a task for. It is also important to remove distractions, have everything you need for your task to hand and break big tasks into smaller ones.

And when trying to remember things more efficiently, why not write lists or post-it notes with things you need to remember to do? Alternatively, use memory techniques to help you remember things, like mnemonics, rhymes and sensory reminders, such as associating the thing to remember with a visual image, smell or sound. And when trying to remember more in-depth information, such as that needed for exams, make sure you:

- understand the information you are trying to remember
- associate it with real-life things, as that can aid memory
- learn it in ways that work for you either through visual learning (learning through seeing), auditory learning (learning through hearing) or kinaesthetic learning (learning through doing).

Now that you have learned about several different ways in which you can change how you think in order to starve your Depression Gremlin and manage your depression, it's time to focus on how you can also act differently to achieve the same results – which is what the next chapter is all about.

12

Acting Differently!

In Chapter 6, we learned that we act in ways that aren't good for us when we are experiencing depression and that these self-defeating behaviours feed our Depression Gremlins and make our depression worse.

But we don't have to act in these ways. We can choose to act differently, by:

Reducing our self-defeating behaviours	Implementing more constructive behaviours

Acting differently will help to starve your Depression Gremlin and get your depression under control, as changing what we *do* can help change how we *feel*!

Remember, you don't have to try all the different strategies that you learn in this chapter. You only need to apply those that are relevant to you.

Reducing Self-Defeating Behaviours

The first way to change how you act is to reduce the behaviours that aren't good for you.

STOP AVOIDING!

Many people with depression avoid or escape from certain situations or avoid doing certain things, such as solving problems or making decisions. Or they may quit or give up part way through doing activities or give up on activities before they have even tried. They can also become dependent on other people doing things for them instead of doing them themselves or hide away from other people. This can be because of:

- a lack of motivation or interest
- not experiencing any sense of enjoyment or pleasure from situations and activities any more
- fear or worry about what might happen
- viewing situations as threatening or scary
- a sense of hopelessness
- a lack of confidence.

Avoiding situations can also be a way of avoiding experiencing unpleasant feelings in response to them.

But, avoidance only makes us feel worse. When we face these situations instead, we give ourselves the opportunity to see that there is a difference between how we think and feel about a situation and what actually happens in it. For example, we get to see that:

- the negative outcomes that we are predicting are unlikely to come true
- we can achieve those things that we keep telling ourselves we can't, thus allowing our confidence to grow
- we can cope even if our worst-case scenario does happen
- it is OK to experience unpleasant feelings sometimes
- we can simply let unpleasant feelings go or work out the best way of responding to them.

Therefore, it is important to ***gradually*** put yourself into the situations that you would normally avoid or escape from or quit or give up on due to your depression, and eventually your depression will reduce. Psychologists call this...

gradual exposure.

But, take it step by step. Start with tasks or situations that seem easiest, such as going into your back garden for some fresh air, and only move onto the next step, such as going on a five-minute walk, when you feel ready. Accept that you will feel some worry, fear or stress at first, as that is normal. But, remind yourself that it will pass. If you feel unable to do one of the actions, try breaking it down into smaller steps and tackle those bit by bit. It is OK to need to repeat a step several times until you feel completely comfortable with it.

If you are struggling to motivate yourself to complete the steps, remind yourself of why you need to, the benefits it will bring and that it will be OK. And remember that if we wait for our motivation to come back before we do things, we will never do anything when depressed. Instead, we must ***make ourselves*** take those first steps and, if we keep doing things, ***eventually*** we will feel more comfortable doing them and our motivation to continue and our desire to do other things as well will return.

Also, use the realistic thinking techniques that you learned in the previous chapter along with other behavioural strategies that you will learn later in this chapter (for example, relaxation techniques) to help you along the way. Finally, reward and praise yourself for achieving each step.

STOP PROCRASTINATING!

We often put off doing certain activities when suffering with depression and waste time doing other things instead, like watching TV. When we put off doing something, we call this...

procrastination.

Just like avoidance, procrastination stops us from seeing that things aren't as bad as we think they are and from realising that we can cope and achieve! To starve your Depression Gremlin, you need to reduce procrastination by:

- thinking realistically and positively about the activity you are putting off and your ability to complete that activity using the techniques that you learned in the previous chapter
- stopping making excuses for why you can't start or complete the activity
- visualising yourself successfully achieving the activity
- starting the activity that you are putting off
- setting yourself a step-by-step plan containing realistic and achievable steps towards completing the activity and tackling each step one at a time
- reducing the opportunity to get distracted by other things
- reminding yourself of the disadvantages of procrastination, such as not giving yourself enough time to complete the activity
- reminding yourself of the advantages of reducing procrastination, such as allowing yourself to see that you can achieve what you need to achieve
- reminding yourself of times when you didn't procrastinate and how well it went
- rewarding yourself along the way for completing steps off your plan and for achieving your final goal!

BECOME ASSERTIVE

As human beings, we all have certain rights, including the rights to:

- be treated with respect
- say, 'No!'
- have choice

- be listened to
- not be physically harmed by others
- express our opinions
- ask for help.

When you are assertive, you recognise that your rights are equal to those of other people, you respect your own rights and the rights of others, and you stand up for your rights, needs and values. However, people with depression can behave in ways that are...

passive or aggressive.

Passive behaviours are behaviours that indicate you:

- believe that your rights are less important than the rights of others
- doubt yourself and your abilities
- believe that you are unworthy
- believe that your opinions, needs, wishes and feelings do not matter
- worry about upsetting or not pleasing others
- worry about something bad happening.

And, as a result, they feed your Depression Gremlin, making your depression worse. Here is one young person's story as an example.

CHRIS'S STORY

Chris, aged 15 years, found his depression worsening because he was so overwhelmed by all he was trying to do to please his parents and meet their high expectations. He felt like he never had any time to himself, to rest or to just hang out with his friends because he had a class or club to go to every evening and weekend. He didn't want to attend them all but didn't feel he could say 'No!' to his parents as he didn't want them to be disappointed in him.

Passive behaviours include:

- avoiding giving your opinion or agreeing with the opinion of others on a regular basis, even though you don't agree with them
- avoiding expressing your feelings, wishes or needs
- acting in ways to please others all the time
- being unable to say 'No!' to others on a regular basis
- frequently saying 'Sorry', even when you have done nothing wrong
- frequently saying things like 'I think...but I might be wrong' or 'I think...but it's only my opinion'
- frequently putting yourself down when you speak
- frequently dismissing your thoughts, opinions, feelings, wishes and needs as unimportant when you speak, such as 'I wanted to do... but it doesn't matter'
- not addressing the situation when another person denies your rights completely or treats them as less important than theirs
- avoiding any form of disagreement or conflict.

Passive behaviour also involves the use of passive body language in our interactions with other people. Our body language includes our:

- tone of voice
- level of eye contact
- posture
- gestures
- facial expressions.

Passive body language can include:

- avoiding eye contact
- quiet or soft tone of voice
- head down or looking down
- fidgeting or twitching
- hunched shoulders
- clearing throat frequently
- crossing arms for protection
- wringing hands
- trembling
- lip biting.

Here is another example of one young person who feeds her Depression Gremlin with passive behaviours.

KEESHA'S STORY

Keesha is 11 years old. She has no confidence in herself or her abilities. She doesn't see herself as important or worthy, so will always put the needs of others before her own needs. A group of girls verbally bully her most days at school. She hasn't told anyone, as she doesn't see why anyone would care about her, and she doesn't stand up for herself, as she doesn't think she's strong enough to do so. Her dad screams and shouts at her at home and tells her she is a waste of space and he wishes she had never been born. She has never told anyone outside of the family home and just puts up with it. Over time, she has come to hate herself more and more, sees herself as weak and pathetic and doesn't see the point of her existence. Keesha is severely depressed.

Answer the questions in the Depression Box on the next page about your own passive behaviours.

DEPRESSION BOX

My passive behaviours include:

. . . .

. . . .

. . . .

. . . .

. . . .

Passive body language that I regularly use includes:

. . . .

. . . .

. . . .

. . . .

. . . .

Advantages of acting in passive ways include:

. . . .

. . . .

. . . .

. . . .

. . . .

Disadvantages of acting in passive ways include:

. . . .

. . . .

. . . .

. . . .

. . . .

Some people experiencing depression will act in aggressive instead of passive ways. Such aggressive behaviours can include:

- treating another person with disrespect
- putting down the other person
- verbal abuse
- shouting at the other person
- pushing your opinion on someone else
- meeting your needs and wishes at the expense of demanding your own way

- dismissing or ridiculing the opinions, thoughts and feelings of others
- dictating what another person can say or do
- threatening another person
- being physically aggressive towards another person
- taking anger and frustration with yourself out on someone else.

Aggressive body language can include:

- raised tone of voice or shouting
- staring or glaring
- fist clenching
- pointing
- scowling
- entering the other person's personal space.

A person with depression can also act in aggressive ways towards themselves due to the anger and frustration that he or she experiences in response to their overly negative or unrealistic thoughts about themselves.

Here is an example of one young person whose depression comes out as aggression.

NOEL'S STORY

Noel is 12 years old. He was taken into care at the age of five due to his mum's drug and alcohol problems. He has always blamed himself, thinking he must have been a bad son for his mum to have not wanted him. He has always struggled to make friends, as he doesn't believe anyone would ever like him. He doesn't see the point of his life and often has suicidal thoughts. He has so much hate towards himself built up inside of him that he takes it out on other people around him. He screams and shouts at his foster parents, frequently breaks and destroys things within the home and gets into fights at school over the tiniest of things. Noel is severely depressed.

Acting in aggressive ways towards yourself or others will feed your Depression Gremlin, thus worsening your depression.

If you ever act in such ways, answer the questions in the Depression Box that follows on the next page.

DEPRESSION BOX

My aggressive behaviours towards others include:

....

....

....

....

The aggressive body language that I use towards others includes:

....

....

....

....

My aggressive behaviours towards myself include:

....

....

....

....

Advantages of acting in aggressive ways include:

....

....

....

....

Disadvantages of acting in aggressive ways include:

....

....

....

....

The key way to overcome passive and aggressive behaviours is to learn about being assertive. Assertiveness will help you to starve your Depression Gremlin!

When you are assertive, you:

- Recognise that your rights are equal to those of others
- Respect the rights, feelings, opinions, wishes and needs of others
- Believe that your thoughts, feelings, needs and wishes matter and express them in a calm and respectful way
- Stand up for your rights in a calm and respectful way
- See yourself as worthy
- Believe in yourself

Have a go at answering some of the questions about your assertiveness in the Depression Box below.

DEPRESSION BOX

List any situations that you feel you are assertive in.

....

....

....

In what types of situations would you like to be more assertive?

....

....

....

How do you think you could achieve this?

....

....

....

To be assertive you need to:

- *Think and speak assertively* – thinking and speaking in ways that show you believe in yourself and don't involve putting yourself down, such as using phrases like 'I believe' instead of 'I'm probably wrong'
- *Act assertively* – such as listening to the other person; acknowledging the other person's point of view in a respectful way (but without having to agree with it); expressing your point of view in a calm, respectful and confident way; saying 'No!' to others when you need to; calmly dealing with disagreements or conflict; calmly standing up for your rights; and offering potential solutions to problems in a calm, respectful and confident way
- *Use assertive body language* – which can include good eye contact, relaxed and confident posture, body language that indicates you are listening, such as leaning forward slightly, and speaking in a clear, calm and firm tone (not overly loud or overly quiet) and at a steady pace (not too quickly).

These assertiveness skills will help you to:

- show other people that you believe in yourself and value yourself
- have the confidence to make your own choices
- have the confidence to act in situations
- say 'No!' in response to unrealistic pressures or demands
- put your point of view across
- express your feelings, needs and wants
- ask for help
- deal with people who are disrespectful to you
- deal with bullying or conflict
- reach resolutions and compromises

- respond to constructive criticism in an appropriate manner
- give constructive criticism
- improve your communication skills
- improve your relationships with others
- feel proud of yourself
- believe in yourself
- starve your Depression Gremlin
- reduce your depression.

Think about the last time you acted in either a passive or aggressive way due to your negative or unrealistic thoughts and feelings about yourself, then answer the questions in the Depression Box that follows.

DEPRESSION BOX

The situation was:

....

....

How did I think about the situation and myself?

....

....

How did I feel about the situation and myself?

....

....

How did I behave?

....

....

Were my thoughts assertive? Tick which answer applies to you.

YES ☐ NO ☐

If no, how could I have thought more assertively?

....

....

Were my behaviours assertive? Tick which answer applies to you.

YES ☐ NO ☐

If no, how could I have behaved more assertively?

....

....

Would thinking and behaving assertively have brought better results? Tick your answer.

YES ☐ NO ☐

Where possible, it can help to think through how you could respond to a situation more assertively in advance. It can also help to visualise yourself being assertive in the situation beforehand. You can also practise assertive body language in front of a mirror or an assertive tone of voice using a voice recorder.

REDUCE OTHER SELF-DEFEATING BEHAVIOURS

This would be an incredibly long workbook if I was to go through everything that is needed to tackle all the other self-defeating behaviours that were listed in Chapter 6, such as:

- seeking reassurance from others or needing to be around others for comfort
- defiant, disruptive or risk-taking behaviours
- restless behaviours
- using negative coping strategies, such as drinking alcohol, using drugs, self-harming, skipping meals or binge eating.

However, setting yourself a gradual plan for reducing the frequency and amount of the behaviour that you want to tackle is a good place to start, as these behaviours feed your Depression Gremlin, making your depression worse. For example, alcohol and drug use can negatively affect your judgement and mood.

The next few pages have some strategies that can help with reducing your self-defeating behaviours.

DITCH THOSE TOOLS!

Reduce the opportunity to perform the behaviour by removing the tools you need to achieve it. For example, if you wish to reduce binge eating, stop buying the foods you would binge on.

DISTRACT YOURSELF!

Distract yourself from performing the behaviour by doing something else instead. The best forms of distraction are things that you enjoy doing, things that give you a sense of achievement, things that calm you, and things that really absorb your attention.

DELAY, DELAY, DELAY!

Wait a little while before you start to perform the behaviour, as by waiting, even for just five minutes, it can reduce the urge to perform the behaviour. You are showing yourself that you have a choice over whether and when you perform this behaviour. You can also use the delay time to work on challenging any negative or unrealistic thoughts using the realistic thinking methods from the previous chapter!

SAY 'STOP!'

Say a trigger word like 'stop!' to yourself when you feel the urge to perform the behaviour. This gives you the opportunity to challenge any negative or unrealistic thoughts using the realistic thinking methods discussed in the previous chapter.

SET LIMITS!

Place limits on your behaviours to restrict them in some way. This can include setting limits for the number of times you perform the behaviour in a day or a week or for the time you spend performing the behaviour. It can also include only allowing yourself to perform the behaviour at a set time each day, and if you miss that time you must wait until the next day.

IS IT WORTH IT?

Write yourself a list of the advantages and disadvantages of performing the behaviour.

RESISTANCE!

Resist the urge to perform the behaviour completely. You may be able to do this straight away for behaviours that you don't believe are as vital or that you haven't been doing for as long. But for those you have the strongest urge for, you may have to build up to this more gradually using some of the other techniques outlined here.

NO!

OUT WITH THE OLD AND IN WITH THE NEW!

Replace the behaviour with a more constructive way of acting, such as those we will look at in the rest of this chapter.

SAFETY!

If one of your self-defeating behaviours is self-harming, it is important that whilst you are working out ways to reduce this behaviour, you ensure you perform it safely. This can include:

* not using dirty items to harm yourself with
* using safer methods, such as an ice cube on your skin, pinching your skin, pinging an elastic band on your wrist, marking your skin with body paint or squeezing a stress ball

* taking care of any injury you may cause and, if necessary, seeking medical assistance for an injury through your school nurse, GP or hospital.

You are likely to feel increased levels of worry or fear at first when trying to reduce your behaviours in these ways. But this is normal and will gradually reduce, especially if you implement one or more of the constructive behaviours that we will look at in the rest of this chapter.

In the worksheet that follows, answer the questions about a self-defeating behaviour that you want to reduce first. You can use the Self-Defeating Behaviours Worksheet to help you reduce any other self-defeating behaviours you may have as well.

Self-Defeating Behaviours Worksheet

Please write or draw your answers to the questions in the spaces below.

My self-defeating behaviour is...

The advantages of my self-defeating behaviour are...

The disadvantages of my self-defeating behaviour are...

I can reduce my self-defeating behaviour by...

Implementing Constructive Behaviours

When people are depressed, they tend to behave in accordance with their feelings. But, we can change how we act by implementing more constructive behaviours instead of self-defeating ones. Doing this will help us to:

- relax
- feel better physically, mentally and emotionally
- be more confident
- build up our motivation levels
- reintroduce feelings of enjoyment and pleasure
- cope with life pressures
- take our mind off negative thoughts or reduce the time available to us for thinking negatively
- starve our Depression Gremlin
- get our depression under control!

The constructive behaviours that we are going to look at are:

- talking
- pretending
- using the 'worry time' technique
- completing a thoughts, feelings and behaviours diary
- changing your self-talk
- showing yourself kindness and compassion
- increasing your activity levels and having fun
- relaxing
- living healthily

- problem solving
- improving relationships and social skills
- having ambitions.

But remember, you don't need to use them all. Only use those that you believe will help you to starve your Depression Gremlin! Try them out, repeat them several times and see which work best for you by looking at their effects on your mood. But don't try too much at once. Take it step by step so as not to scare or overwhelm yourself.

TALKING

Talking with a person that you trust is an important way of managing your depression and starving your Depression Gremlin, as it can help you to:

challenge your negative and unrealistic thoughts

express how you are feeling and get help with dealing with negative emotions

keep safe if you are experiencing suicidal thoughts (see Chapter 13 for more information if you are experiencing suicidal thoughts)

identify ways to solve problems or cope with situations

Don't forget, you can also talk to a professional, such as a GP, psychologist, psychiatrist, counsellor or therapist, about your depression and the ways it is affecting you, as well as any life difficulties that may be triggering your depression. You can also contact a telephone helpline or access their online chat services or join a face-to-face or online support group to speak about how you are feeling and to obtain support. Please see Appendices 1 and 2 for some useful contacts.

PRETENDING

Acting as if you are feeling better, even if you don't, can often help to motivate you into doing other things that will benefit you and your mood.

USING THE 'WORRY TIME' TECHNIQUE

People experiencing depression often experience worry or anxiety alongside it, which can worsen feelings of depression. 'Worry time' is a specific time in the day that you can use to think, talk or write about the things that you are worrying about and how you can think and act differently to get this worry under control. But set a time limit, as it defeats the purpose of 'worry time' if it lasts all day!

Reducing your worries and anxiety can have a positive effect on your mood and can help to starve your Depression Gremlin! Please see *Starving the Anxiety Gremlin: A Cognitive Behavioural Therapy Workbook on Anxiety Management for Young People* (Collins-Donnelly 2013) for more information on how to manage anxiety.

You can also use 'worry time' to practise the mindfulness techniques discussed in the previous chapter and let your negative thoughts and feelings go!

COMPLETING A THOUGHTS, FEELINGS AND BEHAVIOURS DIARY

Writing your thoughts, feelings and behaviours down on paper can help you to challenge any negative and unrealistic thoughts you might be having and to identify ways of acting differently to help you manage your depression or resolve a problem you might be facing. A diary to complete can be found below. You can also use this diary during 'worry time' to address any worries you might be experiencing.

Thoughts, Feelings and Behaviours Diary

Write or draw your answers to the questions in the spaces below.

Date:

What was the situation?

What were your thoughts?

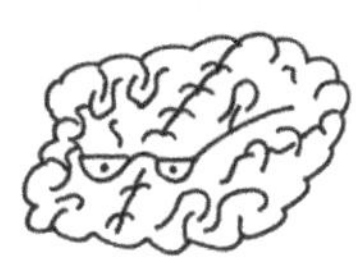

Did you think through Depression Thinking Glasses? Tick which answer applies to you.

YES ☐ NO ☐

What physical reactions did you experience?

How did you feel emotionally?

How did you act?

Did you feed or starve your Depression Gremlin? Tick your answer.

FEED ☐ STARVE ☐

If you fed him, what could you have done differently to starve him?

If you starved him, well done!

CHANGING YOUR 'SELF-TALK'

Your self-talk is how you talk about yourself. Being aware of how you talk about yourself and your abilities will help you to starve your Depression Gremlin and get your depression under control. Your self-talk needs to be realistic and positive, just as your thoughts do. Have a go at answering the questions in the following Depression Box to help you identify what your own self-talk is like and how you can change this for the better.

DEPRESSION BOX

What words do you currently use when talking about yourself and your abilities?

....

....

....

....

What effects does your self-talk have on you?

....

....

....

....

How could you improve your self-talk?

....

....

....

....

SHOWING YOURSELF KINDNESS AND COMPASSION

Remember to also show yourself kindness and compassion as part of your self-talk.

You have always had the power to starve your Depression Gremlin and get your depression under control, but until you picked up this workbook, you may not have known how. So instead, you have acted in the ways that seemed the best thing to do at the time, including the various self-defeating behaviours that we discussed in Chapter 6. Even though they haven't actually helped in the long term, you did the best you could at the time and no-one can ever judge you or criticise you for that. And you shouldn't judge or criticise yourself for it either.

Q. If one of your friends was struggling to cope with something in their life, which of the following would you do? Tick your answer.

Criticise them ☐ Show them understanding and support ☐

I'm guessing you chose the understanding and support option, and you would be right to do so. And this understanding and support is what we mean when we talk about compassion. So why not show yourself this same compassion? It's OK to struggle sometimes. You are not a failure if you do. And you shouldn't beat yourself up about it.

By understanding that it's OK to struggle sometimes, by showing yourself compassion and by letting go of the urges to criticise yourself for the situation you have ended up in, you will free yourself up to focus on starving your Depression Gremlin. So, be kind to yourself and encourage and praise yourself!

INCREASING YOUR ACTIVITY LEVELS AND HAVING FUN!

It is common for people experiencing depression to:

stop doing things they used to enjoy and be interested in

reduce their activity levels in general

stop many parts of their usual daily routines

stop socialising with others

This is because symptoms of depression include a loss of energy, enjoyment, pleasure, motivation, interest and confidence, alongside feeling like everything is hopeless or overwhelming. It can feel easier to just give up. But then you aren't giving yourself the opportunity to have positive experiences and see just how well you can do. You are also preventing the return of your enjoyment and motivation. And being inactive or spending too much time alone or without things to do:

- leads you to feel worse physically
- makes it harder for you to sleep
- gives you more time to think negatively about yourself, thus increasing negative emotions, such as shame.

Therefore, even though it may feel too hard, an important way to starve your Depression Gremlin is to increase your activity levels. Psychologists and therapists call this...

behavioural activation or activity scheduling.

As Albert Einstein once said:

> *'Life is like riding a bicycle. To keep your balance, you must keep moving.'*

So, although you might not feel motivated to increase your activity levels at first, it is vital that you grit your teeth and make yourself do more with your time. If you do, you will:

- gradually feel more and more comfortable with what you are doing
- feel proud of yourself
- feel more confident
- gain a greater sense of achievement and pleasure
- get structure back into your day
- find that your motivation to continue will kick in!

You need to keep doing and achieving to help the motivation and enjoyment to return. So, gradually increase:

ASPECTS OF DAILY ROUTINES

such as eating, cooking, showering, household chores, going to school, doing homework, having a part-time job, volunteering, etc.

FUN ACTIVITIES

such as sports or exercise, listening to or playing music, drawing, painting, singing, dancing, watching TV, reading, writing, going to the cinema or other leisure activities

SOCIAL ACTIVITIES

such as spending time with friends or family who are happy and fun to be around – not draining – hopefully giving you the chance to smile and laugh with others!

And why not look for ways of meeting new people too?

It is usually easiest to begin with increasing home-based activities or restarting activities you used to do before. You can then introduce new activities or activities outside the home when you feel ready. Sometimes, when people are depressed, they force themselves to do things they think they 'have' to do, such as homework and chores, and let the fun things stop instead. So, look to include activities that:

- give you a sense of achievement and purpose
- make you smile and laugh
- give you something to look forward to
- relax and calm you
- energise or inspire you
- boost your confidence
- help others
- make you feel closer to others
- you are passionate about
- show you positive things about you
- are good for your health and wellbeing
- you can use as an alternative to self-defeating behaviours.

Remember to take small steps – don't rush into too much too soon. But once you feel ready to do so, including a positive and pleasurable activity each day will really help. Also, reward yourself for your achievements. This can include praising yourself, watching your favourite TV programme, eating a favourite food, reading a favourite book, etc. In the Depression Box on the next page, write a list of what your rewards could be.

DEPRESSION BOX

My rewards

Don't beat yourself up if you don't feel able to do an activity that you set for yourself. Just assess why this is the case and work out what you can do to change this.

Throughout the process, keep reminding yourself of the benefits of increasing your activity levels and the disadvantages of giving up on having a full and enjoyable life! The more motivated you are, the more you will enjoy life again, the more you will starve your Depression Gremlin and the better your mood will become!

Use the My Activity Levels Worksheet that follows to help you identify:

- your current daily activity levels
- the daily routine, fun and social types of activities you have stopped doing

- the daily routine, fun and social types of activities that you wish to restart or increase, and where you can fit them into your week
- how your mood changes with increases in your activity levels
- which types of activities make you feel better
- which types of activities make you feel worse.

My Activity Levels Worksheet

CURRENT DAILY SCHEDULE

Use the daily schedule that follows to keep a record of the activities that you currently do each day. You can photocopy this page, so you have enough copies for every day. Write down the day of the week, each activity you do and the time you did it.

Then for each activity tick if:

* it gives you a sense of pleasure
* it gives you a sense of achievement
* it is important to you in some way
* it gives you a sense of closeness to other people.

Finally, put either a ☺ or a ☹ depending on what your mood is like as a result of this activity.

DAY OF THE WEEK:

TIME	ACTIVITY	SENSE OF PLEASURE	SENSE OF ACHIEVEMENT	IMPORTANT TO ME	SENSE OF CLOSENESS TO OTHERS	MOOD

WHAT YOUR DAILY SCHEDULE SHOWS YOU

Which of the activities made you feel worse and why? How can you eliminate or reduce these activities where possible or how can you cope better with them?

ACTIVITIES THAT MADE ME FEEL WORSE	REASON	HOW I CAN ELIMINATE OR REDUCE THE ACTIVITY OR COPE BETTER WITH IT

Which of the activities made you feel better and why?

ACTIVITIES THAT MADE ME FEEL BETTER	REASON

Now list any of the following types of activities that you have stopped doing because of your depression in the spaces below.

DAILY ROUTINE ACTIVITIES	FUN ACTIVITIES	SOCIAL ACTIVITIES

NEW DAILY SCHEDULE

Now list any of the following types of activities that you wish to start, restart or increase in the spaces below.

DAILY ROUTINE ACTIVITIES	FUN ACTIVITIES	SOCIAL ACTIVITIES

Now start making any changes you need to make to your daily activities levels based on what you have learned and monitor the effects of them on your mood on a day-by-day basis using copies of this worksheet.

Don't forget to tick if:

* it gives you a sense of pleasure
* it gives you a sense of achievement
* it is important to you in some way
* it gives you a sense of closeness to other people.

Finally, put either a ☺ or a ☹ depending on what your mood is like as a result of this activity.

DAY OF THE WEEK:

TIME	ACTIVITY	SENSE OF PLEASURE	SENSE OF ACHIEVEMENT	IMPORTANT TO ME	SENSE OF CLOSENESS TO OTHERS	MOOD

RELAXING

You are not on your own if you feel restless, tense, worried, panicky, agitated or irritable when depressed. If you do, you can use simple relaxation and deep-breathing exercises to help you relax and feel calmer. They provide what mindfulness practitioners call...

breathing spaces

...a time to just focus on your breath and body and to take a break from constant streams of thoughts in your head. These can also be helpful when you are trying to face situations that you would normally avoid, or when you want to stop procrastinating or reduce other self-defeating behaviours as discussed earlier in this chapter.

Have a go at the following relaxation and breathing exercises and see what you think. It's OK if these don't feel right to you, as they aren't always suitable for everybody.

DEEP BREATHING EXERCISE 1

Either sit down or lie down on your back. Focus on your breathing. Put one hand on your upper chest and one on your abdomen (just below your ribs). Gently breathe in, and as you do so, notice that your abdomen rises slowly under your hand. Slowly breathe out, noticing how your abdomen falls down slowly. Repeat the process, breathing in and out with a slow, steady rhythm. You are breathing correctly if the hand on your abdomen moves up and down slowly but the hand on your chest remains still. Focus on your breathing only and let your mind clear.

DEEP BREATHING EXERCISE 2

Repeat Exercise 1. But this time, breathe in for a count of 4, breathe out for a count of 8 and then hold your breath without strain for a count of 4. Keep repeating this process – focusing on your breathing only and letting your mind clear.

DEEP BREATHING EXERCISE 3

Lie on your back. Breathe in deeply and slowly imagine that the breath is a life force coming in through the soles of your feet, travelling up through your body and exiting through your head. Breathe in again and this time imagine that the breath is a life force coming in through your head, travelling down through your body and out through the soles of your feet. Repeat this exercise several times and slowly – again focusing only on the movement of your breath.

DEEP BREATHING EXERCISE 4

Sit cross-legged. Breathe steadily in and out for a few times. Then breathe in through your left nostril as you hold in your right nostril with your finger. Then breathe out through your right nostril as you hold in your left nostril with your finger. Repeat several times, focusing on nothing other than the breath – thus clearing your mind and calming your body and emotions.

DEEP BREATHING EXERCISE 5

Do the same as Exercise 4, but this time breathe in through your right nostril and out through your left. Again, repeat several times, focusing on nothing other than the breath. This breathing exercise is designed more for energising you.

DEEP BREATHING EXERCISE 6

Either sit down or lie down on your back. Focus on your breathing. Gently breathe a third of the way in, stopping the breath as it reaches your belly. Pause for a moment, holding the breath in. Breathe in another third of the way – this time stopping as the breath reaches your rib cage. Pause for another moment, again holding the breath in. Finally inhale the rest of the way. Focus on how you feel as you pause each time. Notice how the pauses help you to clear your mind. Repeat this several times and then return to your normal breathing.

VISUALISATION EXERCISE

Close your eyes and imagine yourself somewhere peaceful, happy or enjoyable – somewhere that makes you feel relaxed and happy. Focus on that image, start to build the detail and, for a short time, imagine that you are actually there. Breathe deeply and slowly as you do.

If thoughts pop into your head during any of these exercises, just let them go and focus your attention back on your breathing or the visualisation.

If these breathing and relaxation activities aren't for you, you can always try other forms of activity or exercise that are aimed at relaxation, such as meditation, yoga and T'ai Chi. Alternatively, you can use other activities that you enjoy to help you relax, such as listening to chilled music, reading a good book, watching a 'feel good' film, etc.

LIVING HEALTHILY

When we are depressed, our relationship with food can go a bit haywire as our appetite can decrease or we can be prone to comfort eating unhealthy foods. Our sleep can also be poor, and we can lack the motivation and energy to look after our personal hygiene and appearance and to exercise. This feeds our Depression Gremlin further, has a negative effect on our mood and keeps us trapped in the vicious cycle of depression. For example, if we don't exercise, we are unlikely to sleep as well, leading us to:

- feel worse physically and emotionally
- think in more negative and unrealistic ways
- do even less activity – further worsening our sleep.

But, all these areas can be improved upon to help you starve your Depression Gremlin.

DIET

It is important to eat a healthy balanced diet, have regular meals and reduce your sugar and junk food intake, as poor diet can lead to surges and drops in blood sugar, which can impact negatively upon our mood and energy levels. Eating the wrong foods, comfort eating or not eating enough can also all lead to a drop in energy and mood levels.

Also, drink plenty of water, as our brains work better when properly hydrated, and reduce the amount of stimulants you drink, like caffeine and sugary drinks.

PERSONAL HYGIENE AND APPEARANCE

It is important to take care of your personal hygiene and appearance no matter how unmotivated you feel, as it will help you to feel better about yourself and more confident and will give you a sense of achievement.

EXERCISE

Exercise regularly, as exercise releases 'feel-good chemicals' in the brain, known as endorphins, that can help to improve mood, energy and motivation. Exercise can also help to:

* release any tension or stress
* distract from negative thoughts and improve thought processes
* improve appetite, sleep and general fitness and health, including helping to maintain healthy bones, joints and muscles, boost the immune system, improve circulation, reduce blood pressure, reduce fat levels and improve skin condition
* give a sense of achievement
* improve confidence.

But exercise at a pace that is right for you. Start slowly and build up gradually. Perhaps start with a form of exercise that you used to do or pick a new type that you believe will suit you. Exercising with others could improve your motivation to continue with the exercise as well as improving your social life. Also, doing stretches can help with the physical aches and pains of depression.

SLEEP

It is also important to get enough quality sleep. Why not try some of the following sleep hygiene techniques if you are having trouble sleeping because of your depression?

Bed is for sleep

For some people, making sure their bed is only used for sleep, and not for activities like watching TV or using a computer, can help improve their sleep.

Sleep environment

Look at what changes you may need to make to your sleep environment, such as noise levels, light levels, colours in the room, types of bed/mattress, heat levels and distractions in the room (for example, mobile phones or TV). Your bedroom needs to be a restful, uncluttered, comfortable and calm place. There is also evidence emerging about how improving the air quality in your room may help to improve sleep, such as through the use of Himalayan salt lamps.

Pre-bed routine

Avoid anything too stimulating before bed. Do things that help you to relax instead. Empty your bladder before bed to reduce the chance of waking up in the night. Don't use electronic devices like laptops, tablets and mobile phones for at least 30 minutes prior to bedtime, as research shows that the blue light emitted by them disrupts our body clocks, making sleep harder. Use 'worry time' to deal with any negative thoughts or problems prior to bed. If negative thoughts or worries keep popping into your head, remind yourself that you have already dealt with them and let them go. If new ones appear, write them down in a notebook by your bed ready to deal with them in the morning.

Sleep routine

Get up at approximately the same time each day using an alarm clock and avoid daytime naps, including at weekends. Go to bed at approximately the same time each day as well. Choose a time for this when you would normally feel sleepy. Signs of sleepiness can include yawning, itchy eyes and struggling to keep your eyes open. You can always try making your bedtime later if you continue to struggle to fall asleep. Some people have a sleep routine that is backwards – i.e. they sleep in the day and are awake at night. If this is the case for you, try moving your bedtime and waking times forward by an hour each day until you return to night-time sleeping.

Exercise

Ensure you have done some physical activity in the day, but don't do aerobic exercise too close to bedtime, as your body will be too stimulated to sleep.

Eating

Eat at regular times, as our body clock is also influenced by eating times. Also avoid food too close to bedtime, as the digestion process can keep you awake, and avoid stimulants like caffeine, as they can disturb sleep patterns too. Caffeine is found in tea and coffee and in some soft drinks and chocolate snacks. Also, nicotine from cigarettes can keep people awake, and while alcohol may initially make people feel sleepy, it is likely to disturb a person's sleep throughout the night.

Daylight

It's important to experience natural daylight every day as this stimulates the sleep hormone called melatonin.

If you still can't sleep

People who sleep well tend to fall asleep within approximately 20 minutes of getting into bed. So, if you can't get to sleep, get out of bed after 20 minutes and do something relaxing, and when you feel tired go back to bed and try to sleep again. Turn your clock to the wall, as looking at it will only make you feel worse. Don't worry about not being able to sleep – this will only make things worse, as how we think about sleep impacts on the quality of sleep we get.

Nightmares

Nightmares are only dreams, and dreams only become nightmares when we have a frightened response to them. If you notice that certain things trigger off your nightmares, such as watching specific TV programmes or eating certain foods close to bedtime, please avoid these. Also, dealing with any worries or stresses in your life can help reduce nightmares, as can the other sleep hygiene techniques that have already been discussed. Another useful strategy is to remember the nightmare if you can, then write out a more positive version of it and regularly visualise that positive version. And it also helps to remember that dreams don't predict the future.

PROBLEM SOLVING

Difficult situations and problems are a normal part of life. But, when we are experiencing depression, it can feel like the problems are all our fault, too much to cope with and unsolvable, which leaves us overwhelmed, anxious and stressed. The result is often procrastination or avoidance, including pretending the problem doesn't exist or getting someone else to deal with the problem for us.

Stressing or worrying about difficult situations and problems and avoiding dealing with them will not make them any better and will only feed your Depression Gremlin and make your depression worse. Instead, you need to challenge any negative thinking and focus your energy on practical ways to solve the problem you are facing in order to starve your Depression Gremlin and improve your mood. The more you practise problem solving, the easier you will find it, and your confidence will grow, helping your depression to reduce.

When working out how to tackle a problem, you need to:

- identify exactly what the problem is
- make sure the problem is a *real* one in the *here and now*, not an imaginary one or one from the past that cannot be solved, or one that you are imagining might occur in the future
- think about possible solutions to the problem
- look at the pros and cons of each solution
- decide which solution to take
- plan out how to do it
- visualise yourself solving the problem or role play solving it if this will be helpful
- put your plan into action

- review how it went
- try another solution if your first choice doesn't work
- reward yourself.

Sometimes, you might not feel ready to do what you need to do to solve the problem. If so, accept this, give yourself a break and then tackle it when you feel stronger. This does not make you weak and neither does asking for help with problem solving when you need to.

Also, remember that we cannot solve every problem in life. In some cases, we have to accept that we have no control over the problem or that there are things in life that we cannot change, such as other people's behaviours. But we can control our reaction to the situation facing us and find ways to cope with it, even if we can't resolve it completely. Just by accepting this, we are changing our response, and that is what helps. Sometimes, the best way forward is to just let something go instead of battling against it or constantly thinking about it. This isn't you giving up or being weak. This is you making a sensible choice under the circumstances.

IMPROVING RELATIONSHIPS AND SOCIAL SKILLS

Difficulties in the important relationships in our lives can also have a negative impact upon our mood. So it is beneficial to identify these difficulties and how we can resolve them. To help with this, try answering the questions in the Depression Box on the next page about a relationship that you are currently having difficulties with.

DEPRESSION BOX

Who is the relationship with?

. . . .

What are the positives about this relationship?

. . . .

. . . .

. . . .

. . . .

What are the negatives about this relationship?

. . . .

. . . .

. . . .

. . . .

What expectations are you placing on this relationship?

. . . .

. . . .

. . . .

What would you change about this relationship, and how could these changes be achieved?

. . . .

. . . .

. . . .

Our mood can also be low if we have difficulties with:

- understanding what friendships are
- how to make new friendships
- how to keep existing ones going.

To help with this, answer the questions in the Depression Box below, as learning more about positive relationships and how to achieve them can help you to starve your Depression Gremlin and get your depression under control.

DEPRESSION BOX

What does the word 'friendship' mean to you?

....

....

....

What should a positive friendship involve or be like?

....

....

....

How can you be a good friend to others?

....

....

....

What could you do to make new friends?

....

....

....

....

What can help to keep friendships going?

....

....

....

....

If you struggle with how to interact with other people – known as social skills – it can help to practise different social scenarios, such as:

- starting conversations
- keeping conversations going
- meeting new people and introducing yourself
- talking to people you already know and people that you don't
- listening to others
- complimenting others
- joining in in groups and working with others
- giving your opinion
- asking for help
- dealing with conflict.

You can write out scenarios and what you would do on paper, or you can visualise them in your head or role play them. It is also important to practise your skills in real-life situations too when you feel ready. And why not see if your school offers any social skills training courses that you could go on that will help you with such situations and give you the opportunity to learn more about verbal communication skills and non-verbal ones, such as body language and tone? You can also look for books or apps that can help you to develop your social skills further.

HAVING AMBITIONS

When we are depressed, it is easy to see things in life as hopeless, pointless and bleak. Therefore, to help you starve your Depression Gremlin, it is important to think about your ambitions for the future. Think about what you want to achieve in the future and what you want your future to be like. Then work out what steps you need to take to achieve this and act on them. But don't just get focused on the end goal – you must enjoy getting there too. As Arthur Ashe, a former professional tennis player, once said:

> *'Success is a journey, not a destination. The doing is often more important than the outcome!'*

In the Depression Box that follows, set yourself at least five things you want to achieve in the future and what steps you can take now to help you achieve these ambitions.

DEPRESSION BOX

MY AMBITIONS	STEPS I CAN TAKE TO ACHIEVE THEM

Well done! You have learned so much to help you starve your Depression Gremlin and get your depression under control! Now, it is about putting it all into practice at a pace and in a way that feels right for you!

13

Knowing What to Do if You Are Feeling Suicidal

Some people experiencing depression can have what we call...

suicidal thoughts.

These are thoughts about ending your life, such as thinking life is so hopeless you don't want to continue living or thinking that others would be better off if you were dead.

When we are feeling very low, it is understandable that we can sometimes think this way, and as you will have seen from Chapter 8, you are not on your own in having such thoughts. But as overwhelming and as scary as they can feel, you must remember...

They are just thoughts like any other thought!

You don't have to act on them!

The thoughts will pass.

You can overcome them.

And there are people who can help you.

If you have thoughts about ending your life, it is vital that you get help straight away to keep you safe. Remember, you are not on your own. This chapter looks at the types of people you can speak to for help and other ways you can keep yourself safe if you have suicidal thoughts.

Be Aware of Your Triggers and Warning Signs

There may be certain things, places, people, etc. that tend to *trigger* your suicidal thoughts. If so, be aware of these and try to stay away from them where possible until you have obtained professional support to help you overcome your emotional difficulties.

You may also have certain ways that you tend to think, feel or act before your suicidal thoughts kick in. These are your...

warning signs.

When you recognise these signs in yourself, putting some of the strategies that follow into practice can help prevent suicidal thoughts developing and reduce any urges to act upon them.

Delay

Delay any decision to act upon your suicidal thoughts. You don't need to act on your thoughts now and you don't have to do something just because you think it. You have a choice as to how you act in response to your thoughts and you can choose to seek help instead. By waiting, the urge to act on your thoughts is likely to reduce and you give yourself the time to get the crisis support you need. You may feel unable to cope right now, but in a few hours or a few days, you may start feeling more able to cope again. Give yourself the chance to see this. Just focus on getting through today one tiny step at a time, instead of thinking about your future.

Speak To an Adult You Trust

Many young people worry that, if they talk to someone about their suicidal thoughts, they:

- won't be taken seriously
- will be judged
- will be told off
- won't be understood
- won't know what to say
- will cause too much worry or upset.

But it is so important to talk to an adult you trust, like a parent, other relative or teacher, about how you are feeling as soon as possible to gain the help and support you need. They can help keep you safe and help you find positive ways to cope and deal with what is troubling you.

If you don't feel like you can talk to someone you know well, then consider talking to your GP, who can put you in contact with counselling support or crisis support services in your area that can provide urgent help where needed. Don't be afraid to ask your GP surgery for an emergency appointment if required or, if it is out of hours, the GP surgery's answer service should provide another number you can call for out of hours help. Alternatively, in the UK, you can call 111 outside of your GP surgery's opening hours and they will be able to put you in touch with the appropriate crisis support services. Also, if you are already receiving support from a Community Mental Health Team or a Crisis Team, you can call them and they can arrange the urgent help you need.

Contact a Helpline

If you don't feel ready to talk to someone you know, then another alternative is to contact one of the helplines on the following pages where you can speak confidentially to someone who is trained in providing the support you need. Their counsellors/advisors want to keep you safe, will never judge you, won't be shocked by what you have to say and will take you seriously. They will understand how hard it is to talk and will give you the time and space to do so. Don't worry if you don't know what to say, as they will help you through this, but they will never pressurise you to talk about anything you don't want to. However, the more you share with them, the easier they will find it to help you.

IN THE UK

ChildLine: Helpline and counselling for young people up to 19 years of age.

Call the confidential 24-hour helpline for free on 0800 1111 to speak to a counsellor. You don't need credit on your phone and it won't show up on your phone bill.

Chat confidentially online with a counsellor at www.childline.org.uk/talk/chat/pages/onlinechat.aspx.

Register at www.childline.org.uk/login/?returnPath=%2flocker%2finbox%2f so that you can send an email to a counsellor. You will get a reply within 24 hours.

For further information on accessing ChildLine support, click on the following webpage: www.childline.org.uk/get-support.

Papyrus HOPELineUK: For young people under 35 years of age experiencing suicidal thoughts.

Call the confidential helpline for free on 0800 068 4141 to speak to an advisor. Opening hours are 10am to 10pm Monday to Friday and 2pm to 10pm on weekends and bank holidays.

Email pat@papyrus-uk.org and an advisor will contact you within 24 hours.

Text 07786 209697 and an advisor will contact you as soon as they can.

For further information on accessing Papyrus support, click on the following webpage: www.papyrus-uk.org/help-advice/about-hopelineuk.

Samaritans: Provides confidential support for whatever is troubling you whatever your age for people in the UK and Ireland.

Call the confidential 24-hour helpline for free on 116 123 to speak to a trained volunteer. You don't have to give any personal information if you don't want to and the advisor cannot see your phone number on their phone.

Email jo@samaritans.org and a volunteer will reply to you, usually within 24 hours. The volunteer cannot see your email address.

Visit a Samaritans local branch to speak to someone in person. Go to www.samaritans.org/branches to find your local branch.

For further information on accessing Samaritans support, click on the following webpage: www.samaritans.org/how-we-can-help-you/contact-us?gclid=EAIaIQobChMIybmLm4ew2gIVzbXtCh0gGQpiEAAYASAAEgI_o_D_BwE.

Shout: A free 24/7 text service for anyone in crisis anytime, anywhere in the UK. It can help with issues such as suicidal thoughts, bullying, relationship issues, abuse, assault and self-harm.

Text SHOUT to 85258 in the UK to text with a trained Crisis Volunteer about any type of crisis you are facing to help you reach a calmer state. We will always try to respond to texters as quickly as possible, however our responses will be longer at times of high demand. We will always respond to high risk texters as a priority.

For further information, click on the following webpage: https://www.giveusashout.org

---

The Mix: Helpline and counselling for young people under 25 years of age.

Call the confidential helpline for free on 0808 808 4994. Opening hours are 11am to 11pm every day.

Speak to the helpline via webchat at www.themix.org.uk/get-support/speak-to-our-team. Opening hours are 11am to 11pm every day.

Email the helpline at www.themix.org.uk/get-support/speak-to-our-team/email-us and you will be contacted within 24 hours.

Text THEMIX to 85258 to access their Crisis Messenger text service if you have an urgent issue, such as suicidal thoughts, self-harm, abuse, assault, bullying, etc. You will be replied to in less than 5 minutes and will be provided with support via text. This service is free and anonymous on the mobile phone networks of EE, O2, Vodafone, Three, Virgin Mobile, BT Mobile, giffgaff, Tesco Mobile and Telecom Plus.

For further information on accessing The Mix support, click on the following webpage: www.themix.org.uk/get-support/speak-to-our-team. To be assessed to see if you are eligible for free telephone or webchat counselling sessions, please contact the helpline using one of the methods above. For further information see www.themix.org.uk/get-support/speak-to-our-team/telephone-counselling or www.themix.org.uk/get-support/speak-to-our-team/the-mix-counselling-service.

WORLDWIDE

USA

Crisis Text Line: Provides free, 24/7 support for people in any type of crisis.

Text 741741 from anywhere in the US to text with a trained Crisis Counsellor.

For further information on accessing Crisis Text Line support, click on the following webpage: www.crisistextline.org.

National Suicide Prevention Lifeline: The National Suicide Prevention Lifeline provides free and confidential emotional support to people in suicidal crisis or emotional distress 24 hours a day, 7 days a week, across the United States.

Call the Lifeline for free on 1-800-273-8255 (English speaking) or on 1-888-628-9454 (Spanish speaking).

Chat with a counsellor online using Lifeline Chat at https://suicidepreventionlifeline.org/chat.

For further information on accessing the National Suicide Prevention Lifeline support or to access helpful resources for young people, click on the following webpage: https://suicidepreventionlifeline.org.

Australia

Lifeline: Lifeline is a national charity providing all Australians with access to 24-hour crisis support and suicide prevention services.

Call Lifeline on 13 11 14, 24 hours a day, 7 days a week.

Access Crisis Support Chat (an online chat service) from 7.00pm to midnight (Sydney time) 7 days a week at www.lifeline.org.au/get-help/online-services/crisis-chat.

Lifeline Text is a trial service. Text 0477 13 11 14 between 5.00pm and 9.00pm (Adelaide time), 7 days a week.

For further information on accessing Lifeline support or to access helpful resources, click on the following webpage: www.lifeline.org.au.

Samaritans: Provides crisis support 24 hours a day, 7 days a week.

Call 135 247 for anonymous crisis support.

Email support@thesamaritans.org.au for help and support.

For further information on accessing Samaritans support, click on the following webpage: www.thesamaritans.org.au.

Suicide Call Back service: This is a nationwide service that provides 24/7 telephone, video and online professional counselling to people who are affected by suicide. The service offers crisis support to anyone in Australia who is aged 15 years and older.

Call any time on 1300 659 467.

Sign up for free video or online counselling at www.suicidecallbackservice.org.au/phone-and-online-counselling.

You may be eligible to receive up to six free telephone counselling sessions, scheduled at times to best suit your needs.

For a range of helpful resources, click on the following webpage: www.suicidecallbackservice.org.au/resources/feeling-suicidal. For further information on contacting the Suicide Call Back service, click on the following webpage: https://www.suicidecallbackservice.org.au.

Distract Yourself

Do something to distract yourself from your suicidal thoughts. Activities that fully absorb your attention or that you gain some sense of positivity or achievement from are the best ones to try.

Exercise and Relax

If you feel able, do some form of exercise, as exercise helps to release 'happy hormones' in the body, such as serotonin and dopamine, and it is a great form of distraction from suicidal thoughts.

Also try doing something that you find relaxes you, such as breathing exercises, meditation, yoga, reading, listening to music, watching a particular film, etc.

Visualise

Think about something that makes you feel happy or safe or that makes you laugh.

Positives List

List the things about you and your life that are positive and all the things you have to look forward to and/or that are worth living for. It's important to keep reminding yourself of these reasons for living.

Be Around Others

When you are experiencing suicidal thoughts, it is important to avoid being alone, as this will reduce the opportunity for you to act on your thoughts. Be around people until your suicidal thoughts reduce. This could be people you know like friends or relatives, or it could be going to a public place, such as a shopping centre, café or library.

Go to Your Safe Place

Identify a place in which you feel safe, such as a friend or relative's house or a local church, community centre, library, café, etc., and go there if you can get there safely.

Ditch the Tools

Get rid of any items that you might use to harm yourself, such as prescription medication, over-the-counter medication or razor blades. Give them to someone you trust until you feel more able to cope.

Stay Away from Drugs and Alcohol or Anything Else That Makes You Feel Worse

Do not consume any alcohol or illegal drugs. Alcohol can affect our judgement and can have a depressant effect on our mood – thus putting us at a greater risk of acting on suicidal thoughts. It can also make some people more irritable or angrier.

Drugs can also affect our judgement and the way we feel, with some making us more likely to take risks, others causing confusion and paranoia, others causing hallucinations and others making us feel low either whilst on them or after their effects have worn off. All of this can put a person using drugs at greater risk of acting on suicidal thoughts.

You may find that being in certain places, listening to certain songs, watching certain films, etc. when you are already having suicidal thoughts make you feel worse. If so, again you must try to avoid these.

Emergency Help

If you are in real danger of taking your life or if you have just made a suicide attempt, call 999 (UK), 911 (USA and Canada) or 000 (Australia) immediately and ask for an ambulance/paramedics or go straight to your local Accident and Emergency Department/ Emergency Room. Get someone else to call for you or take you if needed.

Make a Safety Plan

It is important to use the ideas and information in this chapter to create a safety plan for yourself that you can follow step by step if you experience suicidal thoughts. This is a plan that will help to keep you safe and to starve your Depression Gremlin.

Answer the questions in the Safety Plan Worksheet that follows on the next few pages to create your own safety plan. You can obviously design this in any way you like and add anything else you wish. Always keep a copy of your safety plan with you or nearby.

Safety Plan Worksheet

Write your answers to the questions in the spaces below, or on a separate piece of paper, in a notebook or on your phone/tablet if you prefer.

Who could I contact?

	NAME	CONTACT DETAILS
ADULTS I TRUST		
PROFESSIONALS		
HELPLINES		

What can I do to…

DISTRACT MYSELF?	RELAX?	GET EXERCISE?

What could I tell myself? (e.g. my thoughts are only thoughts and I don't have to act on them)

What could I visualise?

What are my reasons for living?

Who could I be around?

Where can I go to feel safe?

What things should I avoid as they make me feel worse?

What should I remove from my house/room/bag?

If I feel suicidal and out of control, I need to:

* go to the nearest Accident and Emergency Department/Emergency Room
* call 999 (UK), 911 (USA and Canada) or 000 (Australia).

This safety plan will keep me safe and help me to starve my Depression Gremlin.

14

Summing Up!

Congratulations! You have now learned what you need to know about depression and how to starve your Depression Gremlin. It's now down to you to put your learning into practice. But don't forget, you may not need to use all the strategies we've looked at in this workbook. Just work on implementing those that are relevant to you and your own depression.

Remember, only you can change how:

- you think about yourself, your life and life events, your future, other people and the world around you
- your body reacts physically as a result of your thoughts
- you feel emotionally in response to your thoughts
- you act in response to your thoughts and feelings!

You have the power to starve your Depression Gremlin

and get your depression under control!

Just believe in you!

As the famous quote goes:

> *'Let your smile change the world, but don't let the world change your smile.' (Unknown)*

To help you believe in your ability to starve your Depression Gremlin, let's have a quick recap using some activities.

What Have You Learned?

First, write down five things you have learned about depression and how to control it in the Depression Box below.

DEPRESSION BOX

What I have learned about depression and how to control it

Spread the Word on How to Starve the Depression Gremlin!

Now have a go at a more creative way of reinforcing what you have learned with the following activity.

YOUR VOICE! (PART 2)

If you wanted to spread the word far and wide to other young people about depression and how to manage it, what would you do? Pick whether you would:

* design a webpage for young people to access
* write a blog aimed at young people
* design a poster campaign for schools and colleges
* design scenes for a TV advert
* give a talk at schools and colleges
* deliver a play at schools and colleges.

Then, in the space on the next page, jot down ideas on the kinds of things you would include in whichever type of campaign method you would use. And if you want to have a go at completing your campaign on some separate paper or a computer, go ahead. Just think, maybe your school or college might want to use it!

Teaching other young people about depression

Depression Agony Aunt or Uncle

Jessie is 13 years old. She suffers with a medical condition called Ulcerative Colitis, which causes her to have severe stomach pain, frequent trips to the toilet and diarrhoea. She feels embarrassed when she has to ask to leave lessons to go to the toilet several times in a school day. Other pupils at school make fun of this and some call her nasty names.

Jessie spends a lot of time thinking that she is useless and pathetic and often asks herself what the point of living is when her life involves such pain, discomfort and people being mean to her. Jessie feels so humiliated by her condition that she doesn't socialise with her friends any more after school. She has stopped leaving the house other than for school, as she is worried about not having access to a toilet when out. Jessie has also started to scratch at her arms and legs until they bleed as a way of dealing with all the horrible emotions she has built up inside of her. Jessie feels so tired all the time, but she cannot sleep at night. She rarely showers, eats very little and speaks nastily to her family. Jessie feels like she is sinking under the weight of her dark emotions.

What advice would you give Jessie to help her starve her Depression Gremlin and manage her depression? Write your advice in the next Depression Box.

DEPRESSION BOX

Dear Jessie...

Depression Changes

In the Depression Box below, write down any changes you have seen in your mood since starting this workbook and what you think has led to these changes.

DEPRESSION BOX

Changes in my mood and why

Depression Goals

Next, in the Depression Box below, write down any goals you would like to set yourself so you can continue to starve your Depression Gremlin and keep working on getting your depression under control.

DEPRESSION BOX

My depression goals

I hope that you have seen your depression levels start to reduce and that the way you are responding to situations in life is starting to change too. As you continue to put everything you have learned from this workbook into practice, remember to be patient with yourself. You won't change everything overnight and no-one gets it right all the time! Remember, no-one is perfect and the road to recovery is always up and down – just as it is if you are recovering from a physical injury.

Support from Others

Don't forget to ask for help from others when you need to. Sometimes, the people you speak to might not know the best way to help, so why not let them know what you need? In the Depression Box below, write down ways in which you would like others to help and support you. For example, Harley, aged 15 years, who is experiencing depression wrote:

> 'Give me space when I need it.'
>
> 'Listen to me.'
>
> 'Give me hugs.'
>
> 'Help me to come up with alternative thoughts.'
>
> 'Exercise with me.'

You can give a copy of this to the people you want the help from.

DEPRESSION BOX

How I would like others to help and support me

Don't Stop Starving Your Depression Gremlin!

When you do start to feel better, it is important to continue to implement positive and constructive ways of thinking and acting to help prevent you slipping back into depression in the future. Keep doing the things that are helping you to feel better.

To help you with this, why not create a...

Starving Your Depression Gremlin Scrapbook or Box.

You can include the answers to the activities in this workbook, as well as:

- photos, mementos, objects, etc. that help to remind you of the positives about you and your life
- song lyrics, poems, images of or information about people, etc. that inspire you
- anything else that will help to remind you that you are worthy and your life is worth living.

Setbacks are Normal

Remember what things tend to trigger your depression and look out for any warning signs of depression if these triggers occur. But don't worry if you do find your mood lowering again. Don't beat yourself up. Don't despair. Setbacks can happen. What counts is how you pick yourself back up again, as a setback doesn't have to mean you are spiralling back into depression.

So, if you do see symptoms of depression appearing, remind yourself of what works for you to starve your Depression Gremlin and put this into practice again – your depression should become more manageable once more. You can do it!

To help you feel more prepared, just in case of a potential setback, complete the Setback Prevention Worksheet that follows.

Setback Prevention Worksheet

Write or draw your answers to the questions in the spaces below.

What are my trigger situations?

What are my warning signs? (include any thoughts, physical feelings, emotions and behaviours)

What do I need to do to get me back on track and starve my Depression Gremlin again?

Congratulations! You have now completed the full workbook. Just keep putting everything you have learned into practice and your Depression Gremlin will be tiny sooner than you think!

Good luck!

This is to certify that

. . . .

. . . .

has successfully completed the *Starving the Depression Gremlin* workbook and can expertly

STARVE THEIR DEPRESSION GREMLIN!

Information for Parents and Professionals

The Purpose of this Workbook

Starving the Depression Gremlin is a self-help workbook, which aims to help young people manage their depression. It is designed for young people to work through on their own (unguided self-help) or with the support of a parent or a professional, such as a teacher, mentor, teaching assistant or youth worker (guided self-help).

Several studies have highlighted the effectiveness of self-help (bibliotherapy) (e.g. Furmark *et al.* 2009; Loeb *et al.* 2000), including for overcoming depression (e.g. Scogin *et al.* 1990). In particular, cognitive behavioural therapy (CBT)-based self-help has been found to be effective (Gellatly *et al.* 2007; Williams *et al.* 2013).

The self-help materials included in this workbook are based on the principles of CBT, mindfulness and behavioural activation, but do not constitute a session-by-session therapeutic programme. However, the materials contained in this workbook can be used as a resource for therapists working with young people.

This workbook contains a variety of exercises aimed to help young people get a clearer picture of their depression; however, this workbook does not constitute a diagnostic tool. Self-reporting measures of depression that can be used with young people in clinical practice include:

- Children's Depression Inventory for young people aged 7–12 years (Kovaacs 1982)
- Beck Depression Inventory for Youth for young people aged 7–14 years (Beck, Beck and Jolly 2005)

- Beck Depression Inventory (II) for young people aged 13 years+ (Beck, Steer and Brown 1996)
- Depression Self-Rating Scale for young people aged 9–13 years (Birleson *et al.* 1987)
- Mood and Feelings Questionnaires (MFQ) for young people aged 8–17 years (Costello and Angold 1988)
- Quick Inventory of Depressive Symptomatology – Adolescent Version Self-Report (QIDS-A-SR-17) (Rush *et al.* 2003, 2006).

Depression in Children and Young People

DIAGNOSIS

Depression in children and young people is diagnosed based on the same criteria as adults using either the Diagnostic and Statistical Manual of Mental Disorders (DSM-5) or the International Statistical Classification of Diseases and Related Health Problems (ICD-10). The DSM-5, published by the American Psychiatric Association (APA), provides standard definitions, symptoms and criteria for the classification and diagnosis of mental health disorders. The ICD-10, produced by the World Health Organization, provides standard definitions, symptoms and criteria for the classification and diagnosis of diseases and health issues, including mental health disorders.[1]

PREVALENCE

Rates of anxiety and depression in young people have increased by 70% over the past 25 years (Mental Health Foundation 2004), and the World Health Organization (2014) describes depression as the leading cause of illness and disability in young people. Other studies worldwide have also found increasing levels of depression

1 The different categories of depression detailed in the DSM-5 and their definitions and criteria are detailed in Chapter 3 of this workbook. To see the ICD-10 version 2016 diagnostic criteria, please visit https://icd.who.int/browse10/2016/en#/F30-F39.

among children and young people (e.g. Mojtabai, Olfson and Han 2016; Nuffield Foundation 2013), with many showing that the risk of developing depression increases significantly in adolescence (e.g. Avenevoli *et al.* 2015; Merikangas *et al.* 2010; Public Health England 2016). The latest Good Childhood Report (Children's Society 2018) found that children's happiness is the lowest it has been since 2010 and, of those children and young people who had low happiness with life, 47% also had high depressive symptoms, with 11% reporting high depressive symptoms overall.

A recent national survey of children and young people's mental health in England (Sadler *et al.* 2018) found that 2.1% of children and young people were experiencing a depressive disorder, with this increasing to 4.8% for young people aged 17–19 years. Peru *et al.* (2013) and Birmaher *et al.* (2007) estimate that 2% of children and 6% of adolescents suffer from depression, with lifetime incidence for 3- to 17-year-olds estimated at 4%.

In 2013–14, the ChildLine website pages on 'Depression and feeling sad' received approximately 52,000 views, and their video on depression was viewed more than 24,000 times (NSPCC 2014a). In the same year, young people stated they were depressed in 56% of ChildLine's counselling sessions that related to mental health – this equated to 7194 counselling sessions; and they stated they were feeling suicidal in 20% of the sessions – a rise of 116% compared to 2010–11 (NSPCC 2014a, 2014b). In 2016–17, the top concern raised by young people who contacted ChildLine was mental and emotional health issues, including depression and suicidal thoughts (NSPCC 2017).

Statistics from a YouGov survey of university students published in 2016 found that over a quarter of university students report having a mental health problem, with over three-quarters of these suffering with depression (YouGov 2016). Similar findings were obtained using data gained from the UK Household Longitudinal Survey in 2014–15 where 19% of young people aged 16 to 24 years were found to have symptoms of anxiety or depression (Office for National Statistics 2017).

There is a similar picture worldwide. For example, a national survey in Australia revealed that 1 in 16 young people are currently experiencing depression (Australian Bureau of Statistics 2008), and a survey by Mission Australia (2018) found that, when asked about their happiness levels, approximately 28% of young Australians are 'unhappy or sad' and a further 10% are 'very sad'. In America, a report by the Centers for Disease Control and Prevention (2013) estimated that 2.1% of 3- to 17-year-olds had a current diagnosis of depression. Another American study by Breslau *et al.* (2017) found that depression can start as early as 11 years of age for many young people, and that approximately 14% of boys and 36% of girls had experienced depression by 17 years of age. The 2018 State of Mental Health in America report (Nguyen *et al.* 2018) found that rates of severe depression in 12- to 17-year-olds had risen from 5.9% to 8.2% in a five-year period. Furthermore, approximately 12% report suffering from at least one major depressive episode in the past year, and 63% of those with major depression had not received any mental health treatment (Nguyen *et al.* 2018).

RECOVERY

Studies show that the majority of young people with depression will recover, with 10% recovering after three months, 40% within the first year, and only 20% remaining depressed after two years (Goodyer *et al.* 2003; Harrington and Dubicka 2001).

TRIGGERS

Research continues to highlight how life events can trigger depression. For example, in ChildLine counselling sessions in 2013–14, young people with depression discussed how their depression had been triggered by life events, which included school pressures, bullying, abuse, bereavement and relationship difficulties (NSPCC 2014a). And the reasons given for feeling sad or down by girls aged 7 to 10 years in the Girl Guides Girls' Attitudes Survey were friendship problems, family problems, people at school and school work (Girl Guides Association 2015). The depression experienced by young people in the American study by Breslau *et al.* (2017) was also associated with problems with school and relationships. And in a 2004 study of teenagers aged 13 to 16 years in Ireland who had since recovered from their depression, family problems and bullying were the most common triggers reported (Fitzpatrick *et al.* 2004). The latest Good Childhood Report (Children's Society 2018) also found that 25% of children are subjected to comments and jokes about appearance on a non-stop basis, and that this has a negative effect on their life satisfaction and mental health.

Researchers are also exploring the links between social media usage and depression in young people. For example, Sampasa-Kanyinga and Lewis (2015) found that young people who spend more than two hours per day on social networking sites are more likely to experience mental health issues, including anxiety, depression and suicidal thoughts, and Augner and Hacker (2012) and Lin *et al.* (2016) found that increased or problematic use is associated with significantly increased levels of depression – something that researchers are now terming 'Facebook depression' (American Academy of Pediatrics 2017).

One of the main reasons suggested for this is how young people negatively compare themselves and their lives to those of others that they see on social media sites, including comparing themselves to images that have been digitally manipulated and videos that have been staged. This can lead to a feeling of missing out or inadequacy or a need to be constantly connected with others online because of a fear of missing out – a phenomenon now known as FOMO (Royal Society for Public Health 2017). FOMO has been found to be linked to lower mood and lower life satisfaction (Pryzbylski *et al.* 2013).

Thus, many are arguing that 'the intensity of the online world – where teens and young adults are constantly contactable, face pressures from unrealistic representations of reality, and deal with online peer pressure – may be responsible for triggering depression or exacerbating existing conditions' (Royal Society for Public Health 2017, p.8).

However, it is also important to state that social media can also bring many positive benefits for many young people, including the ability to connect with others and gain support and advice from others in a way that they may not otherwise feel able to do or have access to in everyday life.

SYMPTOMS AND IMPACTS

The symptoms and impacts of depression in young people can vary, but often include low mood, lack of motivation and interest in usual activities, impairments to social and academic functioning, sleep and appetite disturbance, low self-worth and self-confidence, negative thinking, avoidance behaviours, social withdrawal, substance misuse, increased risk for other mental health issues, self-harm and suicide attempts, and increased risk of depression in adulthood (e.g. Hawton, Saunders and O'Connor 2012; Jaffee *et al.* 2002; Naicker *et al.* 2013; Thapar *et al.* 2010).

A 2004 Irish study described how young people used words like 'sad', 'lonely', 'confused' and 'angry' to explain how they felt when depressed, and they also discussed symptoms of hopelessness, isolation, lack of confidence, loss of interest in things, difficulties concentrating, risk-taking and substance misuse (Fitzpatrick *et al.* 2004). A survey of over 5000 young people in schools (Action for Children 2018) found that 33% were struggling, with the most common problems being feeling depressed, difficulty sleeping, inability to shake negative feelings, struggling to 'get going', problems focusing, and feeling like everything is 'an effort'. In ChildLine counselling sessions in 2013–14, young people with depression reported finding it hard to get out of bed in the morning and to face the day ahead (NSPCC 2014a). Some young people talked about suffering in silence as they didn't think they would be taken seriously and about feeling unable to cope, as well as self-harming or feeling suicidal (NSPCC 2014b).

The UK Adult Psychiatric Morbidity Survey in 2007 found that approximately 6% of 16- to 24-year-olds had attempted suicide and approximately 9% had self-harmed (McManus *et al.* 2009). In 2010–11, ChildLine provided 8835 counselling sessions with young people who were thinking about or planning suicide. By 2015–16, this had increased to 19,481 counselling sessions (NSPCC 2016), and by 2016–17, this had reached 22,456 counselling sessions – the highest levels they had ever seen (NSPCC 2017). In 2016–17, 72% of these sessions were with girls (NSPCC 2017), and yet statistics show that more males than females commit suicide (Office for National Statistics 2017).

Suicide is the most common cause of death for boys, and the second most common for girls, aged between 5 and 19 years in the UK (Wolfe *et al.* 2014). In 2014, 149 young people aged 10 to 19 years in England committed suicide (Korkodilos 2016). Worldwide, suicide is the third leading cause of death among adolescents (World Health Organization 2001).

Many young people experiencing suicidal thoughts report feeling unable to tell anyone (NSPCC 2014b) because of a fear that 'other people won't understand what they are going through', or a worry about 'being judged', 'told off' or 'not taken seriously' by their parents (NSPCC 2017, p.38).

From 2001 to 2011, the number of young people admitted to hospital because of self-harm increased by 68% (YoungMinds 2011). In 2006, the Mental Health Foundation stated that between 1 in 12 and 1 in 15 children and young people self-harm. In 2016, Public Health England stated that this was now as high as 1 in 10. The 2018 Good Childhood Report (Children's Society 2018) found that 60% of children with high depressive symptoms had self-harmed.

GENDER, GENDER IDENTITY AND SEXUALITY

Research also highlights the impact of gender, gender identity and sexuality on incidence rates of depression. For example, there are numerous studies that highlight how girls are more likely to experience depression than boys (e.g. Collishaw 2015; Lessof *et al.* 2016; Public Health England 2016; World Health Organization 2017). The UK Household Longitudinal Survey in 2014–15 found that more females than males had symptoms of anxiety and depression (25% and 15% respectively) (Office for National Statistics 2017). This same gender difference was also found in a study by Patalay and Fitzsimons in 2017 where 24% of all girls aged 14 years suffered from depression compared to only 9% of boys of the same age. This equates to approximately 166,000 girls and 67,000 boys nationally (Patalay and Fitzsimons 2017). The 2018 Good Childhood Report (Children's Society 2018) also found that girls had lower life satisfaction than boys and that they were more likely to experience depressive symptoms (16.2%) than boys (5.8%).

Numerous studies are also finding that girls are more likely to self-harm than boys (e.g. Brooks *et al.* 2015). The 2018 Good Childhood Report (Children's Society 2018) also found that girls are twice as likely (22%) as boys (9%) to self-harm.

Research also indicates that LGBT young people are more likely to experience depression than heterosexual young people. For example, the 2018 Good Childhood Report (Children's Society 2018) found that 38% of gay, lesbian or bisexual young people experienced depressive symptoms and 46% had self-harmed. Stonewall's School Report (Guasp 2012) found that 49% of lesbian and bisexual girls and 29% of gay and bisexual boys had symptoms consistent with depression. In addition, 71% of lesbian and bisexual girls and 57% of gay and bisexual boys had experienced suicidal thoughts; 29% of lesbian and bisexual girls and 17% of gay and bisexual boys had made a suicide attempt; and 72% of lesbian and bisexual girls and 36% of gay and bisexual boys had self-harmed (Guasp 2012). A study by the charity METRO (2014) also found that over half of LGBT youth reported self-harm and almost half had considered suicide. LGBT young people who have experienced homophobic bullying are more likely to self-harm, have suicidal thoughts or make suicide attempts, and Guasp (2012) found that 41% of LGBT pupils who had experienced homophobic bullying said that was what had triggered their self-harm. A survey by Nodin *et al.* (2014) found that 48% of transgender people under 26 years of age said they had attempted suicide and 59% had considered doing so, and 59% had self-harmed. A national online survey in Australia also found that 75% of transgender young people had been diagnosed with depression, 79% had self-harmed and 48% had attempted suicide (Strauss *et al.* 2017).

Talking Therapies and Depression

Research highlights the effectiveness of talking therapies in helping to prevent depression and relapses of depression, and in helping with recovery from depression, either as a standalone therapy (e.g. Seligman 1995) or in combination with medication (Elkin *et al.* 1989). Interpersonal psychotherapy has also been shown in research to be effective for the prevention of depression (e.g. Cuijpers *et al.* 2008) as well as for triggering similar positive changes in brain activity to those activated by antidepressants (e.g. Brody *et al.* 2001; Martin *et al.* 2001). Studies are also beginning to highlight its effectiveness as a treatment method for depression in young people (e.g. Mufson *et al.* 2004, 2011; Young, Mufson and Davies 2006; Zhou *et al.* 2015). Family therapy and attachment-based family therapy also show some promising results where the onset of depression is linked to family dynamics and relationships in some way (e.g. Diamond *et al.* 2010; Kolko *et al.* 2000).

CBT, which is one of the treatment approaches that *Starving the Depression Gremlin* is based upon, is the most researched form of treatment for depression. The sections that follow will look at CBT in terms of what it involves and its effectiveness for children and young people and for depression. We will then look at the same areas for mindfulness and behavioural activation – again, treatment approaches that this workbook draws upon.

CBT

What is CBT?

CBT is an evidence-based, skills-based, structured form of psychotherapy, which emerged from Beck's Cognitive Therapy (e.g. Beck 1976) and Ellis' Rational-Emotive Therapy (e.g. Ellis 1962), as well as from the work of behaviourists such as Pavlov (e.g. Pavlov 1927) and Skinner (e.g. Skinner 1938) on classical and operant conditioning, respectively. CBT looks at the relationships between our thoughts (cognition), our feelings (both physical and emotional) and our actions (behaviours). It is based on the premise that how we interpret experiences and situations has a profound effect on our physical, emotional and behavioural reactions.

CBT focuses on:

- the problems that the client is experiencing in the here and now
- why the problems are occurring
- what strategies the client can use in order to address the problems.

In doing so, the CBT process empowers the client to identify:

- negative, unhealthy and unrealistic patterns of thoughts, perspectives and beliefs
- maladaptive and unhealthy patterns of behaviour
- the links between the problems the client is facing and his or her patterns of thoughts and behaviours
- how to challenge the existing patterns of thoughts and behaviours and implement alternative thoughts and behaviours that are constructive, healthy and realistic in order to address problems, manage emotions and improve wellbeing.

Thus, the underlying ethos of CBT is that, by addressing unhelpful patterns of thoughts and behaviours, a person can change how they feel, how they view themselves, how they interact with others and how they approach life in general – thereby moving from an unhealthy cycle of reactions to a healthy one.

A wide range of empirical studies show CBT to be effective with many mental health disorders, including:

- anxiety (e.g. Cartwright-Hatton *et al.* 2004; James, Soler and Weatherall 2005)
- obsessive compulsive disorder (e.g. O'Kearney *et al.* 2006).

Furthermore, guidelines published by the National Institute for Health and Care Excellence (NICE) recommend the use of CBT for several mental health issues.

Effectiveness of CBT for children and young people

Although there has been less research conducted on the use of CBT with children and young people than there has been with adults, evidence for its effectiveness is continuing to grow and being reported in numerous reviews, such as Kazdin and Weisz (1998), Rapee *et al.* (2000) and Weisz and Kazdin (2010). Randomised controlled trials have shown CBT to be effective with children and young people for the following:[2]

- anxiety disorders (Cartwright-Hatton *et al.* 2004), including specific phobias (Silverman *et al.* 1999), generalised anxiety disorder (Kendall *et al.* 1997, 2004) and social phobia (Spence, Donovan and Brechman-Toussaint 2000)
- obsessive compulsive disorder (Barrett, Healy-Farrell and March 2004; Bolton and Perrin 2008)
- school refusal (King *et al.* 1998)
- PTSD (Smith *et al.* 2007).

CBT and depression

CBT has been evaluated as both a standalone therapy for depression and alongside antidepressants. CBT is found to be particularly effective as a standalone treatment for mild-to-moderate depression as well as alongside antidepressant usage (e.g. Butler *et al.* 2006), including for young people (e.g. Brent *et al.* 2008; Curry 2001; David-Ferdon and Kaslow 2008; Klein, Jacobs and Reinecke 2007; Treatment for Adolescents with Depression Study 2004; Watanabe *et al.* 2007; Weisz, McCarty and Valeri 2006; Zhou *et al.* 2015). Studies also highlight the importance of CBT for relapse prevention (e.g. Dobson *et al.* 2008; Hollon *et al.* 2005; Kennard *et al.* 2014) and for the prevention of depressive episodes in at-risk groups of young people (e.g. Garber *et al.* 2009). Although studies in relation to CBT and suicidal risk are still limited, they also show promising results (e.g. Brent *et al.* 2009; Esposito-Smythers *et al.* 2011; Treatment for Adolescents with Depression Study 2007). CBT is therefore a recommended form of therapy for depression (NICE 2009).

---

2 Randomised controlled trials aim to find out which type of treatment or intervention is most effective by making comparisons between different types of treatments or a treatment and either no treatment or a placebo. They are often considered to be the gold standard for clinical trials, with the randomisation process removing any bias.

MINDFULNESS

What is mindfulness?

Mindfulness originates from spiritual disciplines such as Buddhism and from practices such as meditation and yoga. The essence of mindfulness is that we can make a choice to:

- focus our attention on the present moment, thus engaging fully in the here and now with all our senses
- accept our thoughts and feelings as they are, thus observing them without criticism or judgement
- let those thoughts and feelings go, thus reducing any negative impact.

In the 1970s, mindfulness principles and practices were incorporated into a form of training known as mindfulness-based stress reduction (MBSR) developed by Jon Kabat-Zinn. In the 1990s, principles of mindfulness also emerged within psychotherapy and became known as mindfulness-based cognitive therapy (MBCT) for use with people with a history of depression.

The key principles of mindfulness detailed above are also now incorporated into acceptance and commitment therapy (ACT), a mindfulness and values-based form of behavioural therapy. ACT sees our 'private experiences' (namely our thoughts, feelings and physical sensations) as not harmful in themselves. What is seen as harmful within ACT is how we choose to respond to those private experiences, such as seeing them as reality (what ACT terms 'cognitive fusion') and avoiding experiencing these thoughts, feelings and physical sensations (known as experiential avoidance). Thus, as well as teaching us principles of acceptance and being fully present in the moment, ACT also teaches us to make a distinction between our 'private experiences' and reality (a process known as 'cognitive defusion') and to commit to action which enriches and nourishes our lives based upon our values (known as values-consistent behaviours).

The empirical support for ACT as an effective form of treatment for mental health issues such as anxiety and depression is growing (e.g. Forman *et al.* 2007).

Effectiveness of mindfulness-based therapies for children and young people

Research on the use of mindfulness-based therapies with children and young people is still in its infancy. However, evidence supporting its use is growing (e.g. Bogels *et al.* 2008; Semple and Lee 2011), especially in relation to ACT (e.g. Greco *et al.* 2005; Murrell and Scherbarth 2006). Studies are showing support for the use of ACT for children and young people with depression (Hayes, Boyd and Sewell 2011), generalised anxiety disorder (Greco 2002), anorexia nervosa (Heffner, Sperry and Eifert 2002) and pain (Greco *et al.* under review). And research is beginning to highlight how ACT can help to address the links between body image concerns and disordered eating in young people (Greco and Blomquist 2006). Studies are also highlighting the effectiveness of mindfulness-based programmes in schools (e.g. Huppert and Johnson 2010; Joyce *et al.* 2010; Kuyken *et al.* 2013; Napoli, Krech and Holley 2005; Schonert-Reichl and Lawlor 2010; Vickery and Dorjee 2016).

Mindfulness and depression

Research into the effectiveness of mindfulness-based approaches such as MBCT (Williams and Penman 2011) for treating or preventing depression shows positive results. For example, Teasdale *et al.* (2000) and Hofman *et al.* (2010) found mindfulness to be effective in helping to overcome depression, and Piet and Hougaard (2011), Kuyken *et al.* (2008) and Segal *et al.* (2010) found it to be effective at preventing relapses of depression. Furthermore, there are promising results emerging in studies for the use of MBCT with treatment-resistant or chronic depression (e.g. Barnhofer *et al.* 2009; van Aalderen *et al.* 2011). Studies also highlight how school-based mindfulness programmes can have a positive effect on depressive symptoms that students are experiencing (e.g. Joyce *et al.* 2010; Kuyken *et al.* 2013).

BEHAVIOURAL ACTIVATION

What is behavioural activation?

Common symptoms of depression include social withdrawal, inactivity, a lack of motivation and a lack of interest in and pleasure from usual activities. Behavioural activation is a brief, structured, individualised form of therapy for depression that aims to tackle this area. It is based on the idea that what we do affects how we feel. It suggests that by doing more things that we enjoy, value and gain a sense of achievement from, and by reducing how much we act in negative ways, we can help to improve our mood. It also focuses on coping strategies that keep people stuck in the cycle of depression, such as avoidance, and looks at ways of resolving and replacing these through activity and problem solving. Behavioural activation interventions have been part of behavioural and cognitive behavioural treatments, including for depression, for a long time, but it has now gained status as a standalone treatment for depression.

Effectiveness of behavioural activation for children and young people

Research into the effectiveness of behavioural activation with children and young people is still in its infancy. However, emerging studies are showing positive results (e.g. Chu *et al.* 2009; Jacob *et al.* 2013; McCauley *et al.* 2016; Ritschel *et al.* 2011).

Behavioural activation and depression

Research is beginning to highlight the effectiveness of behavioural activation for treating depression, including severe depression, and preventing relapses (e.g. Dimidjian *et al.* 2006; Dobson *et al.* 2008; Ekers, Richards and Gilbody 2008; Jacobson, Martell and Dimidjian 2001). This is also proving to be the case with children and young people (e.g. Chu *et al.* 2009; Jacob *et al.* 2013; McCauley *et al.* 2016; Ritschel *et al.* 2011; Tindall *et al.* 2017). Chartier and Provencher (2013) also found support for the use of behavioural activation in a low intensity form for depression, such as through guided self-help.

Appendix 1

Sources of Help and Support in the UK

Helplines You Can Contact for a Wide Range of Issues

CALM: Confidential support and signposting for males.

Call the helpline for free in London on 0808 802 58 58 or nationwide on 0800 58 58 58. Opening hours are 5pm to midnight every day.

To contact the helpline via webchat, click on www.thecalmzone.net/help/webchat.

For more information, click on www.thecalmzone.net.

ChildLine: Helpline and counselling for young people up to 19 years of age.

Call the confidential 24-hour helpline for free on 0800 1111 to speak to a counsellor. You don't need credit on your phone and it won't show up on your phone bill.

Chat confidentially online with a counsellor at www.childline.org.uk/talk/chat/pages/onlinechat.aspx.

Register at www.childline.org.uk/login/?returnPath=%2flocker %2f inbox%2f so that you can send an email to a counsellor. You will get a reply within 24 hours.

For further information on accessing ChildLine support, click on the following webpage: www.childline.org.uk/get-support.

Community Advice and Listening Line Wales: A confidential listening and support service for anyone concerned about their mental health or the mental health of a loved one.

Call the helpline for free on 0800 132 737. Opening hours are 9am to 6pm Monday to Friday.

Text the helpline on 81066.

For more information, click on www.callhelpline.org.uk.

Kooth: Free, anonymous online support for young people.

Visit https://kooth.com to chat with a counsellor online. Opening hours are 12pm to 10pm Monday to Friday and 6pm to 10pm at weekends. You can send a message online outside of these hours.

Mind Infoline: Information on mental health, treatment options and how to access support.

Call the Infoline on 0300 123 3393. Opening hours are 9am to 6pm Monday to Friday.

Text the Infoline on 86463.

For information on how to access webchat, click on www.mind.org.uk/information-support/helplines/web-chat.

Papyrus HOPELineUK: For young people under 35 years of age experiencing suicidal thoughts.

Call the confidential helpline for free on 0800 068 4141 to speak to an advisor. Opening hours are 10am to 10pm Monday to Friday and 2pm to 10pm on weekends and bank holidays.

Email pat@papyrus-uk.org and an advisor will contact you within 24 hours.

Text 07786 209697 and an advisor will contact you as soon as they can.

For further information on accessing Papyrus support, click on the following webpage: www.papyrus-uk.org/help-advice/about-hopelineuk.

Samaritans: Provides confidential support for whatever is troubling you whatever your age for people in the UK and Ireland.

Call the confidential 24-hour helpline for free on 116 123 to speak to a trained volunteer. You don't have to give any personal information if you don't want to and the advisor cannot see your phone number on their screen.

Email jo@samaritans.org and a volunteer will reply to you, usually within 24 hours. The volunteer cannot see your email address.

Visit a Samaritans local branch to speak to someone in person. Go to www.samaritans.org/branches to find your local branch.

For further information on accessing Samaritans support, click on the following webpage: www.samaritans.org/how-we-can-help-you/contact-us?gclid=EAIaIQobChMIybmLm4ew2gIVzbXtCh0gGQpiEAAYASAAEgI_o_D_BwE.

Sane: Helpline for people 16 years and over.

Call the confidential helpline called SaneLine on 0300 304 7000. Opening hours are 4.30pm to 10.30pm every day.

Shout: A free 24/7 text service for anyone in crisis anytime, anywhere in the UK. It can help with issues such as suicidal thoughts, bullying, relationship issues, abuse, assault and self-harm.

Text SHOUT to 85258 in the UK to text with a trained Crisis Volunteer about any type of crisis you are facing to help you reach a calmer state. We will always try to respond to texters as quickly as possible, however our responses will be longer at times of high demand. We will always respond to high risk texters as a priority.

For further information, click on the following webpage: https://www.giveusashout.org

---

The Mix: Helpline and counselling for young people under 25 years of age.

Call the confidential helpline for free on 0808 808 4994. Opening hours are 11am to 11pm every day.

Speak to the helpline via webchat at www.themix.org.uk/get-support/speak-to-our-team. Opening hours are 11am to 11pm every day.

Email the helpline at www.themix.org.uk/get-support/speak-to-our-team/email-us and you will be contacted within 24 hours.

Text THEMIX to 85258 to access their Crisis Messenger text service if you have an urgent issue, such as suicidal thoughts, self-harm, abuse, assault, bullying, etc. You will be replied to in less than 5 minutes and will be provided with support via text. This service is free and anonymous on the mobile networks of EE, O2, Vodafone, Three, Virgin Mobile, BT Mobile, giffgaff, Tesco Mobile and Telecom Plus.

For further information on accessing The Mix support, click on the following webpage: www.themix.org.uk/get-support/speak-to-our-team. To be assessed to see if you are eligible for free telephone or webchat counselling sessions, please contact the helpline using one of the methods above. For further information see www.themix.org.uk/get-support/speak-to-our-team/telephone-counselling or www.themix.org.uk/get-support/speak-to-our-team/the-mix-counselling-service.

Websites with Mental Health Information for Young People

Children's Society: www.childrenssociety.org.uk/mental-health-advice-for-children-and-young-people

HeadMeds: www.headmeds.org.uk

Mind: www.mind.org.uk/information-support/guides-to-support-and-services/children-and-young-people/#.WykyOfZFw2w

Rethink: www.rethink.org/living-with-mental-illness/young-people

Royal College of Psychiatrists: www.rcpsych.ac.uk/mentalhealth

Teenage Health Freak: www.teenagehealthfreak.org

YoungMinds: https://youngminds.org.uk

Other Sources of Support

BEREAVEMENT

Cruse Bereavement Care: Provides support, advice and information when someone you care about dies.

Call the confidential helpline for free on 0808 808 1677. Opening hours are 9.30am to 5pm on Monday and Friday and 9.30am to 8pm on Tuesday, Wednesday and Thursday.

Email hopeagain@cruse.org.uk and a trained volunteer will reply.

To speak to someone in person, go to www.cruse.org.uk/cruse-areas-and-branches to find your local branch of Cruse Bereavement Care or phone the helpline for details.

For further information on bereavement specifically for young people, including stories from other young people, go to Cruse Bereavement Care's Hope Again website: http://hopeagain.org.uk.

BULLYING

Bully Busters: Helpline providing advice and support in relation to bullying.

Call for free on 0800 169 6928.

Visit www.bullybusters.org.uk/young_people or www.bullybusters.org.uk/kids for more information on bullying.

Bullying UK: Helpline providing advice and support in relation to bullying.

Call to speak to a Family Support Worker on 0808 800 2222. Opening hours are 9am to 9pm Monday to Friday and 10am to 3pm at weekends.

Visit www.bullying.co.uk for more information on bullying.

Ditch the Label: International anti-bullying charity.

Visit www.ditchthelabel.org/get-help to search through thousands of guides and articles on bullying for an answer to your question or to join a community forum and post questions or read the posts of others.

Visit www.facebook.com/DitchtheLabel to send a private message to a digital mentor.

Visit www.ditchthelabel.org/contact to send an email enquiry via an online form.

Call 01273 201129 to speak to someone who can help you to find the information or support you need. Opening hours are 9am to 5.30pm Monday to Friday.

National Bullying Helpline: Helpline providing advice and support in relation to bullying.

Call 0845 225 5787. Opening hours are 9am to 5pm Monday to Friday.

Visit www.nationalbullyinghelpline.co.uk for more information on bullying.

CARERS

Carers Trust: Advice, information and support for carers, including young carers.

For information for young carers, including how to find support organisations in your area, click on the following webpage: https://carers.org/about-us/about-young-carers.

DISABILITY

Mencap: Advice and information for people of all ages with a learning disability.

Call the helpline for free on 0808 808 1111. Opening hours are 9am to 5pm Monday to Friday. Press option 2 if you live in Northern Ireland or Option 3 if you live in Wales.

Email the helpline at helpline@mencap.org.uk, or at helpline.ni@mencap.org.uk if you live in Northern Ireland or at helpline.wales@mencap.org.uk if you live in Wales.

For further information go to www.mencap.org.uk.

Scope: Support for people of all ages with a disability.

Call the confidential helpline for free on 0808 800 3333. Opening hours are 8am to 6pm Monday to Friday.

Email the helpline at helpline@scope.org.uk.

For further information for young people with a disability or to find support in your local area, go to www.scope.org.uk/support/disabled-people/young-disabled.

DOMESTIC VIOLENCE

24-hour National Domestic Violence: A national helpline for women and children experiencing domestic violence.

Call the confidential 24-hour helpline for free on 0808 2000 247.

The Hideout: Website run by Women's Aid providing information for children and young people on domestic violence.

For information on domestic violence, click on http://thehideout.org.uk.

DRUGS AND ALCOHOL

Al Anon: Providing support for the loved ones of alcoholics.

Call the helpline on 020 7403 0888 in England, Wales and Scotland and on 01 873 2699 in the Republic of Ireland. Opening hours are 10am to 10pm every day. Call 028 9068 2368 in Northern Ireland. Opening hours are 10am to 1pm Monday to Friday and 6pm to 11pm at weekends.

To attend an Al Anon meeting, call the helpline or visit https://www.al-anonuk.org.uk/meetings in the UK or in the Republic of Ireland to find your nearest meeting. Please note that there are Alateen groups for young people aged 12–17 years available in some areas of the UK and there are also Family Groups.

Talk to Frank: Provides information and advice about drugs and substance misuse.

Call the 24-hour helpline on 0300 123 6600.

Have a confidential live chat at www.talktofrank.com/livechat. Opening hours are 2pm to 6pm every day.

Email for advice at www.talktofrank.com/contact.

Text a question to Frank on 82111 for the cost of a standard text message.

For further information on drugs and substance misuse, click on www.talktofrank.com.

EATING ISSUES

Beat: Support and information in relation to eating disorders.

Call the Youth helpline on 0808 801 0711. Opening hours are 12pm to 8pm on weekdays and 4pm to 8pm on weekends and bank holidays.

For a live webchat go to www.beateatingdisorders.org.uk/support-services/helplines/one-to-one.

Email the helpline on fyp@beateatingdisorders.org.uk.

For more information on eating disorders or to access online support forums or message boards, go to www.beateatingdisorders.org.uk.

GAMBLING

Big Deal: Information, advice and support for young people experiencing or at risk of problem gambling.

Call the free helpline on 0808 802 0133. Opening hours are 8am to midnight every day.

Have a confidential live chat at www.gamcare.org.uk/frontline-services/netline. Opening hours are 8am to midnight every day.

For further information on gambling issues, click on www.bigdeal.org.uk.

GENERAL

Barnardo's: National children's charity that works with children and young people in relation to disability, mental health, domestic violence, being a carer, living in care, child abuse, child sexual exploitation, offending, homelessness, etc.

Visit www.barnardos.org.uk/what_we_do/our_work/service-search.htm to search for Barnardo's services in your area and what issues they can help you with.

Youth Access: Is an advice and counselling network for young people.

Visit www.youthaccess.org.uk/services/find-your-local-service to find free counselling, information and advice services in your area.

HOUSING, HOMELESSNESS AND RUNNING AWAY

Runaway Helpline: Provides information, help and support for young people thinking of running away, who have run away or who have just returned home.

Call the free 24-hour helpline on 116 000.

Have a confidential live chat at www.runawayhelpline.org.uk/contact-us.

Email for advice at 116000@runawayhelpline.org.uk; they aim to reply within 2 hours.

Text the helpline for free on 116 000; they aim to reply within 1 hour.

For further information, click on www.runawayhelpline.org.uk.

Shelter: Information and advice for young people on housing and homelessness.

Call the free advice line on 0808 800 4444 in England and Scotland. Opening hours are 8am to 8pm on weekdays and 9am to 5pm on weekends. Or call 0345 075 5005 between 9.30am and 4pm Monday to Friday in Wales. In Northern Ireland call the Housing Executive on 034 4892 0900.

Call the free emergency helpline in England if you are homeless or might be homeless soon, have somewhere to stay temporarily but nowhere to call home, if you are feeling overwhelmed by your housing situation or at risk of harm. The number is 0808 164 4660. For emergencies in Northern Ireland outside of office hours, call 028 9504 9999.

Have a confidential live chat in England at https://england.shelter.org.uk/get_help or in Scotland at https://scotland.shelter.org.uk/about_us/contact_us.

Visit a local Shelter service for help and support. To see if there is one in your area in England, click on https://england.shelter.org.uk/get_help/local_services, in Wales click on https://sheltercymru.org.uk/get-advice/advice-near-you.

For further information on housing issues in your country, click on https://england.shelter.org.uk, https://scotland.shelter.org.uk, https://sheltercymru.org.uk/get-advice or http://www.shelterni.org.

LGBTQ+

Stonewall: Information service providing details on rights and issues affecting LGBTQ+ people.

Call the free information line on 0800 050 20 20. Opening hours are 9.30am to 5.30pm Monday to Friday.

Complete the online enquiry form at www.stonewall.org.uk/help-advice/contact-stonewalls-information-service.

For more information visit www.stonewall.org.uk.

Switchboard: Confidential information, support and referral service for LGBTQ+ people.

Call the helpline on 0300 330 0630. Opening hours are 10am to 10pm every day.

Instant message the helpline at https://switchboard.lgbt/help/#.

Email Switchboard at chris@switchboard.lgbt.

For more information visit https://switchboard.lgbt.

LOOKED AFTER CHILDREN (CHILDREN IN CARE OR LEAVING CARE)

Become: Charity providing advice for children and young people in care or leaving care.

Call for free on 0800 023 2033. Opening hours are 10.30am to 5pm Monday to Friday.

Email advice@becomecharity.org.uk.

For more information visit www.becomecharity.org.uk/for-young-people.

Coram Voice: Information, advocacy and support service for children and young people in care or leaving care.

Call for free on 0808 800 5792. Opening hours are 9.30am to 6pm Monday to Friday and 10am to 4pm on Saturday. Please note, Video Call is coming soon!

Email help@coramvoice.org.uk. Or complete the online enquiry form at https://coramvoice.org.uk/young-peoples-zone/getting-touch.

WhatsApp for free using a wifi connection to 07758 670369 or text 07758 670369, which will be charged at your standard text rate.

For more information visit https://coramvoice.org.uk/young-peoples-zone.

SELF-HARM

Harmless: Support, information and training for people who self-harm, their friends and families, professionals and for those at risk of suicide.

Email info@harmless.org.uk.

For more information, including a range of helpful factsheets, visit www.harmless.org.uk.

National Self-Harm Network: An online forum for people who self-harm as well as information for people who self-harm and their friends and families.

For sources of information and to access the online forum, visit www.nshn.co.uk.

Self-Injury Support: Support for females affected by self-harm.

Call the helpline for free on 0808 800 8088. Opening hours are 7pm to 9.30pm Tuesday to Thursday.

Text 07800 472908.

For more information visit https://selfinjurysupportorguk.wordpress.com.

SEXUAL HEALTH

Brook: Information and support for young people about sexual health and relationships.

Visit www.brook.org.uk/your-life to find the answers to many questions about sexual health and relationships.

Visit www.brook.org.uk/find-a-service to find a local Brook service near you where you can see a nurse, counsellor or youth worker face-to-face.

Family Planning Agency: Information and support for young people about sexual health and relationships.

Visit https://sexwise.fpa.org.uk to find information about sexual health.

Visit www.fpa.org.uk/find-a-clinic to find a local Family Planning clinic near you providing advice on sexual health as well as access to contraception and testing and treatment for sexually transmitted infections (STIs).

National Sexual Health Helpline: Confidential advice regarding sexual health issues.

Call the helpline for free on 0300 123 7123. Opening hours are 9am to 8pm Monday to Friday.

VICTIMS OF CRIME

Rape and Sexual Abuse Support Centres (RSASC): Provide free, confidential and non-judgemental support services for victims of rape, sexual assault, sexual abuse and incest.

To see if there is a RSASC in your locality, type Rape and Sexual Abuse Support Centre and the name of your area into a search engine such as Google.

Rape Crisis: Information, advice and support for victims of rape, sexual assault and sexual abuse.

Call the national Rape Crisis Helpline for free on 0808 802 9999 to get confidential support and information on local Rape Crisis services.

Helpline opening hours are 12 noon to 2.30pm and 7pm to 9.30pm every day of the year.

For more information, visit https://rapecrisis.org.uk.

Safeline: Information, support, counselling and signposting onto other services for victims of rape, sexual assault and sexual abuse.

Call the Young People's Helpline for free on 0808 800 5007. Opening hours are Monday, Wednesday and Friday: 10am to 4pm; Tuesday and Thursday: 8am to 8pm; and Saturday: 10am to 12 noon.

Email support@safeline.org.uk to access online support.

Text 07860 027573 (texts charged at your standard rate) to access online support.

For more information on help and support available, visit www.safeline.org.uk.

Victims' Information Service: Confidential advice regarding sexual health issues.

Call for free on 0808 168 9293, 24 hours a day, 7 days a week.

Visit www.victimsinformationservice.org.uk to find information relating to crime, its effects and ways forward, and to search for support services in your area.

Visit www.victimsinformationservice.org.uk/young-victims-crime to find information specifically for young people.

Victim Support: Victim Support provide advice and support to victims of crime.

You can call the confidential Supportline for free on 0808 168 9111, 24 hours a day, 7 days a week.

You can complete an online form to request online support from the Supportline by visiting www.victimsupport.org.uk/help-and-support/get-help/request-support.

Visit https://www.victimsupport.org.uk/help-and-support/young-victims-crime to access information and support options specifically for children and young people.

YOUR RIGHTS AND THE LAW

Just for Kids Law: Provides advocacy and legal support for children and young people.

Call 020 3174 2279 to speak to someone about getting help.

If you need emergency help as you are already at a police station or have been contacted by the police who want to interview you, call the same number during office hours or 07886 755321 out of hours.

Email your enquiry to info@justforkidslaw.org.

Lawstuff: Provides information for children and young people on the rights and laws that affect children and young people in different areas, such as education, crime, family circumstances, etc.

Visit https://lawstuff.org.uk.

Migrant Children's Project: Provides help and support for migrant, asylum-seeking and refugee children in the UK.

Call the Advice Line on 020 7636 8505.

National Youth Advocacy Service: Provides information, advice, advocacy and legal representation for children and young people.

Call their helpline for free on 0808 808 1001. Opening hours are 9am to 6pm Monday to Friday.

Email the helpline at help@nyas.net.

Visit https://youngpeople.nyas.net/index.php/get-in-touch/request-a-callback to request that a helpline advisor calls or emails you back.

Write to FREEPOST NYAS, Tower House, Tower Road, Birkenhead, Wirral CH41 1FF (no stamp needed on the envelope).

Please note, some of the sources of support listed in this Appendix will be able to give you information on support groups and other useful services or projects in your local area.

Appendix 2

Worldwide Helplines

American National Helplines

Childhelp National Child Abuse Hotline: The hotline offers crisis intervention, information, and referrals to thousands of emergency, social service and support resources.

Call confidentially and for free on 1-800-422-4453.

For further information on accessing Childhelp, click on www.childhelp.org/hotline.

Crisis Text Line: Provides free, 24/7 support for people in any type of crisis.

Text 741741 from anywhere in the US to text with a trained crisis counsellor.

For further information on accessing Crisis Text Line, click on www.crisistextline.org.

LGBT National Youth Talkline: The Lesbian, Gay, Bisexual and Transgender (LGBT) Youth Talkline provides telephone, online private one-to-one chat and email peer-support, as well as factual information and local resources for cities and towns across the United States.

Call toll-free on 1-800-246-PRIDE (1-800-246-7743). Opening hours are: Monday to Friday from 1pm to 9pm, *Pacific Time* (Monday to Friday from 4pm to midnight, *Eastern Time*) and Saturday from 9am to 2pm, *Pacific Time* (Saturday from noon to 5pm, *Eastern Time*).

Email: help@LGBThotline.org.

For further information on accessing LGBT National Youth Talkline, click on www.glbthotline.org/talkline.html.

National Suicide Prevention Lifeline: The National Suicide Prevention Lifeline provides free and confidential emotional support to people in suicidal crisis or emotional distress 24 hours a day, 7 days a week, across the United States.

Call the Lifeline for free on 1-800-273-8255 (English speaking) or on 1-888-628-9454 (Spanish speaking).

Chat with a counsellor online using Lifeline Chat at https://suicidepreventionlifeline.org/chat.

For further information on accessing the National Suicide Prevention Lifeline support or to access helpful resources for young people, click on https://suicidepreventionlifeline.org.

Teen Line: a confidential hotline for teenagers which operates every evening from 6pm to 10pm PST. If you have a problem or just want to talk with another teen who understands, then this is the right place for you!

Call 1-800-852-8336 toll free from 6pm to 10pm PST every night.

Text 'TEEN' to 839863 to have a text conversation with a peer counsellor.

Alternatively, click on https://teenlineonline.org/talk-now to download the Teen Talk App (a free iPhone app where teens can get support for whatever they may be dealing with from a trained teen by anonymously posting their issue), to access discussions with other teens on the Message Board or to access other sources of helpful information.

The National Association for Anorexia Nervosa and Associated Disorders (ANAD): Provides the ANAD Helpline offering support, information, referrals and resources for people suffering with eating disorders and their loved ones.

Call the ANAD Helpline on 1-630-577-1330. Opening hours are Monday to Friday, 9am to 5pm, Central Time.

For further information on accessing ANAD's support, click on www.anad.org/our-services/eating-disorders-helpline.

The National Domestic Violence Hotline: confidential and free of cost, the National Domestic Violence Hotline provides lifesaving tools and immediate support to enable victims to find safety and live lives free of abuse.

Call toll-free 24/7 on 1-800-799-SAFE (7233).

To access live chat with a hotline advocate or to access more helpful information click on: https://www.thehotline.org/help.

The National Eating Disorders Association (NEDA): dedicated to supporting individuals and families affected by eating disorders.

Call the toll-free, confidential helpline, Monday - Thursday from 9:00 am - 9:00 pm and Friday from 9:00 am - 5:00 pm (EST) on 1-800-931-2237.

Use Click-to-Chat to speak with a live, trained Helpline volunteer if you prefer instant messaging to speaking on the phone. Available at: https://www.nationaleatingdisorders.org/help-support/contact-helpline.

For crisis situations, text "NEDA" to 741741 to be connected with a trained volunteer at Crisis Text Line.

For further information on accessing NEDA support, click on the following webpage: https://www.nationaleatingdisorders.org/help-support.

The National Runaway Safeline (NRS): Is there to listen whether you are thinking of running away or already have. Their services are confidential and non-judgemental.

Call toll-free 24/7 on 1-800-RUNAWAY or 1-800-786-2929.

Click on www.1800runaway.org/youth-teens to have a live chat 24/7 with a helpline member or to post questions or thoughts to the NRS forum and invite others to share their experiences with you.

Trans Lifeline: Trans Lifeline's Hotline is a confidential and anonymous peer support service run by trans people, for trans and questioning callers.

Call the Hotline 24/7 on 877-565-8860 (US) or 877-330-6366 (Canada).

For further information on accessing Trans Lifeline support, click on www.translifeline.org/hotline.

Your Life Your Voice (provided by Boys Town): Provides the opportunity for young people to speak to a counsellor and access to a variety of online help resources.

Call the Hotline on 1-800-448-3000 (English speaking) or on 1-800-448-1833 (Spanish speaking). Open 24 hours a day, 365 days a year.

Chat with a counsellor over Instant Messaging at www.yourlifeyourvoice.org/pages/ways-to-get-help.aspx#text-info. Opening hours are 6pm to midnight CST Monday to Friday.

Text VOICE to 20121 to speak with a counsellor if you are uncomfortable making a call. Opening hours are 12 noon to 12 midnight CST every day.

For further information on Your Life Your Voice or to access a wide range of online help resources, click on the following webpage: www.yourlifeyourvoice.org/Pages/home.aspx.

Australian National Helplines

1800RESPECT: A national, confidential information, counselling and support service for people impacted by sexual assault, domestic or family violence and abuse.

Call 1800 737 732, 24 hours a day, 7 days a week.

Access online counselling by clicking on www.1800respect.org.au/help-and-support/telephone-and-online-counselling.

For further information on accessing 1800RESPECT support, click on www.1800respect.org.au.

Bravehearts: Provides advice and support to those affected by child sexual assault.

Call the Support Line toll free on 1800 272 831. Opening hours are 8.30am to 4.30pm Monday to Friday AEST (Please note hours vary on public holidays).

For further information on accessing Bravehearts support, click on https://bravehearts.org.au/what-we-do/counselling-and-support.

Butterfly Foundation for Eating Disorders: Operates a National Eating Disorders Support Helpline that includes support over the phone, via email and online.

Call the national helpline on 1800 334 673.

Chat online at https://thebutterflyfoundation.org.au/our-services/helpline/chat-online.

Email the helpline at support@thebutterflyfoundation.org.au.

For more information on accessing Butterfly Foundation for Eating Disorders support, click on https://thebutterflyfoundation.org.au.

Gambler's Help Youthline: Advice and support for young people with gambling issues.

Call 1800 262 376 for advice and support, 24 hours a day, 7 days a week. It's anonymous, confidential and free.

If you prefer to chat online with a counsellor, visit www.gamblinghelponline.org.au for live chat or email support 24/7.

For further information on accessing Gambler's Help Youthline support, visit the following webpage: https://gamblershelp.com.au/get-help/under-25s.

GriefLine: National, confidential and free telephone counselling service for individuals and families experiencing loss and grief.

Call 1300 845 745 (national landline only) or (03) 9935 7400 (national or Metro Melbourne) between midday and 3am, 7 days a week.

Email using an online form at https://griefline.org.au/online-counselling-service. A counsellor will respond within 72 hours.

For further information on GriefLine support, click on https://griefline.org.au.

Headspace: Provides access to health workers through local Headspace centres as well as access to phone and online counselling for 12–25-year-olds.

Call 1800 650 890 to speak to a counsellor 7 days a week from 9am to 1am.

Access online counselling services by clicking on https://headspace.org.au/eheadspace/connect-with-a-clinician.

To search for a Headspace centre near you where you can access health workers, such as a GP, psychologist, social worker, alcohol and drug worker, counsellor, vocational worker or youth worker, click on https://headspace.org.au/headspace-centres.

To access helpful resources for young people click on https://headspace.org.au/young-people/life-issues.

For further information on Headspace, click on https://headspace.org.au.

Kids Helpline: National, free, private and confidential 24/7 phone and online counselling service for young people aged 5 to 25.

Call 1800 551 800 to speak to a counsellor 24 hours a day, 7 days a week. It's free to call – even from mobiles!

To access WebChat Counselling, click on https://kidshelpline.com.au/get-help/webchat-counselling. It's open 7 days a week from 8am to midnight AEST.

Email counsellor@kidshelpline.com.au if you can't get to a phone or prefer to write things down. The inbox is checked from 8am to 10pm daily and a counsellor will read your email and reply with information, questions and suggestions for you.

For further information on accessing Kids Helpline support, click on https://kidshelpline.com.au.

Lifeline: Is a national charity providing all Australians with access to 24-hour crisis support and suicide prevention services.

Call Lifeline on 13 11 14, 24 hours a day, 7 days a week.

Access Crisis Support Chat (an online chat service) from 7pm to midnight (Sydney Time) 7 days a week at www.lifeline.org.au/get-help/online-services/crisis-chat.

Lifeline Text is a trial service. Text 0477 13 11 14 between 5pm and 9pm (Adelaide Time), 7 days a week.

For further information on accessing Lifeline support or to access helpful resources, click on www.lifeline.org.au.

QLife: A national counselling and referral service for people who are lesbian, gay, bisexual, trans and/or intersex (LGBTI).

Call 1800 184 527. Opening hours are 3pm to midnight in your state, every day.

Chat online at https://qlife.org.au.

For further information on accessing QLife support, click on https://qlife.org.au.

Samaritans: Provides crisis support 24 hours a day, 7 days a week.

Call 135 247 for anonymous crisis support.

Email support@thesamaritans.org.au for help and support.

For further information on accessing Samaritans support, click on www.thesamaritans.org.au.

SANE Australia: Provides information, guidance and referrals regarding mental health concerns.

Call the SANE helpline on 1800 187 263 to talk to a mental health professional. Opening hours are weekdays from 10am to 10pm AEST.

Access the online Helpline Chat with a mental health professional by clicking on www.sane.org/get-help. Opening hours are weekdays from 10am to 10pm AEST.

Email the helpline at helpline@sane.org.

Access SANE Forums for information and support 24/7 by clicking on www.sane.org/get-help.

For further information on SANE Australia or to access helpful resources, click on: www.sane.org.

SECASA Youth: The SECASA (South Eastern Centre Against Sexual Assault & Family Violence) Youth website contains information for young people about sexual assault, family violence and relationships.

If you have been sexually assaulted, please contact your nearest Centre Against Sexual Assault. In Victoria, phone 1800 806 292. In the rest of Australia, phone 1800 RESPECT.

To access SECASA Youth information, please click on https://youth.secasa.com.au.

Suicide Call Back Service: A nationwide service that provides 24/7 telephone, video and online professional counselling to people who are affected by suicide. The Service offers crisis support to anyone in Australia who is aged 15 years and older.

Call any time on 1300 659 467.

Sign up for free video or online counselling at www.suicidecallbackservice.org.au/phone-and-online-counselling.

You may be eligible to receive up to six free telephone counselling sessions, scheduled at times to best suit your needs.

For a range of helpful resources, click on www.suicidecallbackservice.org.au/resources/feeling-suicidal.

For further information on contacting the Suicide Call Back Service, click on www.suicidecallbackservice.org.au.

Youth Beyond Blue: Provides information, resources and support for young people dealing with depression and/or anxiety.

Call 1300 224 636, 24 hours a day, 7 days a week to speak to a trained mental health professional.

Chat online from 3pm to midnight (AEST), 7 days a week by clicking on www.youthbeyondblue.com/help-someone-you-know/what-to-do-in-an-emergency/get-immediate-support.

Email via an online form at www.youthbeyondblue.com/help-someone-you-know/what-to-do-in-an-emergency/get-immediate-support. You will hear back from a trained mental health professional within 24 hours.

For further information on accessing Youth Beyond Blue services, click on www.youthbeyondblue.com/home.

Canadian National Helplines

BullyingCanada.ca: Offers information, help and support to everyone involved in bullying – the victim, perpetrator, bystander, parents, school staff and the community at large.

Call toll-free 24/7 on 1-877-352-4497.

Email Support@BullyingCanada.ca.

For further information on accessing BullyingCanada.ca support, click on the following webpage: www.bullyingcanada.ca/portfolio-items/national-24-7-telephone-support-network.

Childhelp National Child Abuse Hotline: Offers crisis intervention, information and referrals to thousands of emergency, social service and support resources.

Call confidentially and for free on 1-800-422-4453.

For further information on accessing Childhelp support, click on www.childhelp.org/hotline.

Kids Help Phone: Provides 24-hour, bilingual, anonymous and confidential phone and online counselling and a referral service for young people across Canada.

Call 1-800-668-6868 to speak to a counsellor 24/7.

Speak to a counsellor via Live Chat at https://kidshelpphone.ca/live-chat.

Text CONNECT to 686868 to speak to a counsellor 24/7.

For further information on accessing Kids Help Phone support or to find local support services, click on https://kidshelpphone.ca.

National Eating Disorder Information Centre (NEDIC): A national toll-free helpline providing information on treatment options and/or support to people affected by disordered eating and related concerns.

Call 416-340-4156 in the Toronto area or 1-866-NEDIC-20 (1-866-633-4220) outside of Toronto. Opening hours are Monday to Friday from 9am to 9pm EST.

For further information on accessing NEDIC support, please click on www.nedic.ca.

Teen Line: A confidential hotline for teenagers which operates every evening from 6pm to 10pm PST. If you have a problem or just want to talk with another teen who understands, then this is the right place for you!

Call 1-800-852-8336 toll-free from 6pm to 10pm PST every night.

Text TEEN to 839863 to have a text conversation with a peer counsellor.

Alternatively, click on https://teenlineonline.org/talk-now to download the Teen Talk App (a free iPhone app where teens can get support for whatever they may be dealing with from a trained teen by anonymously posting their issue), to access discussions with other teens on the Message Board or to access other sources of helpful information.

Trans Lifeline: Trans Lifeline's Hotline is a confidential and anonymous peer support service run by trans people, for trans and questioning callers.

Call the Hotline 24/7 on 877-565-8860 (US) or 877-330-6366 (Canada).

For further information on accessing Trans Lifeline support, click on www.translifeline.org/hotline.

Youthspace.ca: Provides an emotional support online chat and text service for anyone under 30 years of age across Canada.

Have an online chat with a counsellor between the hours of 6pm and midnight PST at http://youthspace.ca.

Text to chat with a counsellor on 778-783-0177.

For further information on accessing Youthspace.ca support, click on http://youthspace.ca.

References

Action for Children (2018) 'One third of 15 to 18-year-olds are suffering from mental health issues.' Action for Children Press Campaigns. Available at: www.actionforchildren.org.uk/news-and-blogs/whats-new/2018/october/one-third-of-15-to-18-year-olds-are-suffering-from-mental-health-issues, accessed on 30 October 2018.

American Academy of Pediatrics (2017) 'Clinical report – The impact of social media on children, adolescents and families.' Available at: http://pediatrics.aappublications.org/content/pediatrics/127/4/800.full.pdf, accessed on 19 February 2018.

Augner, C. and Hacker, G.W. (2012) 'Associations between problematic mobile phone use and psychological parameters in young adults.' *International Journal of Public Health 57*, 2, 437–441.

Australian Bureau of Statistics (2008) *National Survey of Mental Health and Wellbeing: Summary of Results, 2007*. Canberra: Australian Bureau of Statistics.

Avenevoli, S., Swendson, J., He, J.P., Burstein, M. and Merikangas, K.R. (2015) 'Major depression in the national comorbidity survey – adolescent supplement: Prevalence, correlates and treatment.' *Journal of American Academy of Child and Adolescent Psychiatry 54*, 2, 37–44.

Barnhofer, T., Crane, C., Hargus, E., Amarasinghe, M., Winder, R. and Williams, J.M.G. (2009) 'Mindfulness-based cognitive therapy as a treatment for chronic depression: A preliminary study.' *Psychotherapy and Psychosomatics 77*, 319–320.

Barrett, P., Healy-Farrell, L. and March, J.S. (2004) 'Cognitive-behavioural family treatment of childhood obsessive compulsive disorder: A controlled trial.' *Journal of the American Academy of Child and Adolescent Psychiatry 43*, 1, 46–62.

Beck, A., Steer, R.A. and Brown, G.K. (1996) *The Manual for Beck Depression Inventory (BDI-II)*. San Antonio, TX: Harcourt Assessment Inc.

Beck, A.T. (1976) *Cognitive Therapy and Emotional Disorders*. New York: International Universities Press.

Beck, J.S., Beck, A.T. and Jolly, J.B. (2005) *Youth Depression Inventory*. San Antonio, TX: Harcourt Assessment Inc.

Birleson, P., Hudson, I., Buchanan, D.J. and Wolff, S. (1987) 'Clinical evaluation of a self-rating scale for depressive disorder in childhood (Depression Self-Rating Scale).' *Journal of Child Psychology and Psychiatry 28*, 43–60.

Birmaher, B., Brent, D., Bernet, W., Bukstein, O. *et al.* (2007) 'Practice parameter for the assessment and treatment of children and adolescents with depressive disorders.' *Journal of the American Academy of Child and Adolescent Psychiatry 46*, 11, 1503–1526.

Bogels, S., Hoogstad, B., van Dun, L., de Schutter, S. and Restifo, K. (2008) 'Mindfulness training for adolescents with externalizing disorders and their parents.' *Behavioural and Cognitive Psychotherapy 36*, 193–209.

Bolton, D. and Perrin, S. (2008) 'Evaluation of exposure with response-prevention for obsessive compulsive disorder in childhood and adolescence.' *Journal of Behavior Therapy and Experimental Psychiatry 39*, 1, 11–22.

Brent, D., Emslie, G., Clarke, G., Wagner, K.D. *et al.* (2008) 'Switching to another SSRI or to Venlafaxine with or without cognitive behavioural therapy for adolescents with SSRI-resistant depression: The TORDIA randomized controlled trial.' *JAMA Psychiatry 299*, 8, 901–913.

Brent, D., Greenhill, L., Compton, S., Emslie, G. *et al.* (2009) 'The Treatment of Adolescent Suicide Attempters study (TASA): Predictors of suicidal events in an open treatment trial.' *Journal of the American Academy of Child and Adolescent Psychiatry 48*, 10, 987–996.

Breslau, J., Gilman, S.E., Stein, B.D., Ruder, T., Gmelin, T. and Miller, E. (2017) 'Sex differences in recent first-onset depression in an epidemiological sample of adolescents.' *Translational Psychiatry 7*, e1139. Available at: www.nature.com/articles/tp2017105.pdf, accessed on 19 February 2018.

Brody, A.L., Saxena, S., Stoessel, P., Gillies, L.A., Fairbanks, L.A. and Alborzian, S. (2001) 'Regional brain metabolic changes in patients with major depression treated with either Paroxetine or interpersonal therapy: Preliminary findings.' *Archives of General Psychiatry 58*, 7, 631–640.

Brooks, F., Magnusson, J., Klemera, E., Chester, K., Spencer, N. and Smeeton, N. (2015) *HBSC England National Report 2014*. Hatfield, UK: University of Hertfordshire. Available at: www.hbscengland.com/wp-content/uploads/2015/10/National-Report-2015.pdf, accessed on 27 March 2018.

Burstow, P. and Jenkins, P. (2016) 'Growing crisis in children and young people's mental health demands action.' *The Guardian*, 30 November. Available at: www.theguardian.com/social-care-network/2016/nov/30/growing-crisis-in-children-and-young-peoples-mental-health-demands-action, accessed on 19 February 2018.

Butler, A.C., Chapman, J.E., Forman, E.M. and Beck, A.T. (2006) 'The empirical status of cognitive-behavioural therapy: A review of meta-analysis.' *Clinical Psychology Review 26*, 17–31.

Cartwright-Hatton, S., Roberts, C., Chitsabesan, P., Fothergill, C. and Harrington, R. (2004) 'Systematic review of the efficacy of cognitive behaviour therapies for childhood and adolescent anxiety disorders.' *British Journal of Clinical Psychology 43*, 4, 421–436.

Centers for Disease Control and Prevention (2013) 'Mental health surveillance among children – United States, 2005–2011.' *Morbidity and Mortality Weekly Report 62*, 2, 1–35. Available at: www.cdc.gov/mmwr/preview/mmwrhtml/su6202a1.htm?s_cid=su6202a1_w, accessed on 19 February 2018.

Chartier, I.S. and Provencher, M.D. (2013) 'Behavioural activation for depression: Efficacy, effectiveness and dissemination.' *Journal of Affective Disorders 145*, 292–299.

Chief Medical Officer (2014) *Annual Report of the Chief Medical Officer 2013, Public Mental Health Priorities: Investing in the Evidence.* Available at: https://www.gov.uk/government/uploads/system/uploads/attachment_data/file/413196/CMO_web_doc.pdf, accessed on 27 March 2018.

Children's Commissioner for England (2016) *Lightning Review: Access to Child and Adolescent Mental Health Services*, May 2016, London, UK. Available at: https://www.childrenscommissioner.gov.uk/wp-content/uploads/2017/06/Childrens-Commissioners-Mental-Health-Lightning-Review.pdf, accessed on 27 March 2018.

Children's Society (2018) 'The Good Childhood Report 2018'. Available at: www.childrenssociety.org.uk/what-we-do/resources-and-publications/the-good-childhood-report-2018, accessed on 30 September 2018.

Chu, B.C., Colognori, D., Weissman, A.S. and Bannon, K. (2009) 'An initial description and pilot of group behavioural activation therapy for anxious and depressed youth.' *Cognitive and Behavioral Practice 16*, 4, 408–419.

Coid, J.W., Ullrich, S., Keers, R., Bebbington, P. *et al.* (2013) 'Gang membership, violence and psychiatric morbidity.' *American Journal of Psychiatry 170*, 9, 985–993. Available at: www.ncbi.nlm.nih.gov/pubmed/23846827, accessed on 27 March 2018.

Collins-Donnelly, K. (2013) *Starving the Anxiety Gremlin: A Cognitive Behavioural Therapy Workbook on Anxiety Management for Young People.* London: Jessica Kingsley Publishers.

Collishaw, S. (2015) 'Annual research review: Secular trends in child and adolescent mental health.' *Journal of Child Psychology and Psychiatry 56*, 3, 370–393.

Costello, E.J. and Angold, A. (1988) 'Scales to assess child and adolescent depression: Checklists, screens and nets.' *Journal of the American Academy of Child and Adolescent Psychiatry 27*, 726–737.

Cuijpers, P., van Straten, A., Smit, F., Mihalopoulos, C. and Beekman, A. (2008) 'Preventing the onset of depressive disorder: A meta-analytic review of psychological interventions.' *American Journal of Psychiatry 165*, 10, 1272–1280.

Curry, J. (2001) 'Specific psychotherapies for childhood and adolescent depression.' *Biological Psychiatry 49*, 12, 1091–1100.

David-Ferdon, C. and Kaslow, N.J. (2008) 'Evidence-based psychosocial treatments for child and adolescent depression.' *Journal of Clinical Child and Adolescent Psychology 37*, 1, 62–104.

Diamond, G., Wintersteen, M.B., Brown, G.K., Diamond, G.M. *et al.* (2010) 'Attachment-based family therapy for adolescents with suicidal ideation: A randomized controlled trial.' *Journal of American Academy of Child and Adolescent Psychiatry 49*, 2, 122–131.

Dimidjian, S., Hollon, S.D., Dobson, K.S., Schmaling, K.B. *et al.* (2006) 'Randomized trial of behavioural activation, cognitive therapy and antidepressant medication in the acute treatment of adults with major depression.' *Journal of Consulting and Clinical Psychology 74*, 4, 658–670.

Dobson, K.S., Hollon, S.D., Dimidjian, S., Schmaling, K.B. *et al.* (2008) 'Randomized trial of behavioural activation, cognitive therapy and antidepressant medication in the prevention of relapse and recurrence in major depression.' *Journal of Consulting and Clinical Psychology 76*, 3, 468–477.

Ekers, D., Richards, D. and Gilbody, S. (2008) 'A meta-analysis of randomized trials of behavioural treatment of depression.' *Psychological Medicine 38*, 611–623.

Elkin, I., Shea, T., Watkins, J.T., Imber, S.D. *et al.* (1989) 'National Institute of Mental Health Treatment of Depression Collaborative Research Program: General effectiveness of treatments.' *Archives of General Psychiatry 46*, 11, 971–982.

Ellis, A. (1962) *Reason and Emotion in Psychotherapy.* New York: Lyle-Stuart.

Esposito-Symthers, C., Spirito, A., Hunt, J., Kahler, C. and Monti, P. (2011) 'Treatment of co-occurring substance abuse and suicidality among adolescents: A randomized pilot trial.' *Journal of Consulting Clinical Psychology 79*, 6, 728–739.

Fitzpatrick, C., Sharry, J., Guerin, S. and O'Hanlon, K. (2004) 'Learning from Young People Who Have Recovered from Depression.' In C. Fitzpatrick and J. Sharry (eds) *Coping with Depression in Young People: A Guide for Parents*. New York: John Wiley & Sons Ltd.

Forman, E.M., Hoffman, K.L., McGrath, K.B., Herbert, J.D., Brandsma, L.L. and Lowe, M.R. (2007) 'A comparison of acceptance- and control-based strategies for coping with food cravings: An analog study.' *Behaviour Research and Therapy 45*, 1, 2372–2386.

Frith, E. (2016) *CentreForum Commission on Children and Young People's Mental Health: State of the Nation.* Available at: https://centreforum.org/live/wp-content/uploads/2016/04/State-of-the-Nation-report-web.pdf, accessed on 28 March 2018.

Furmark, T., Carlbring, P., Hedman, E., Sonnenstein, A. *et al.* (2009) 'Guided and unguided self-help for social anxiety disorder: Randomised controlled trial.' *British Journal of Psychiatry 195*, 5, 440–447.

Garber, J., Clarke, G.N., Weersing, V.R., Beardslee, W.R. *et al.* (2009) 'Prevention of depression in at-risk adolescents: A randomised controlled trial.' *JAMA Psychiatry 301*, 21, 2215–2224.

Gellatly, J., Bower, P., Hennessy, S., Richards, D. *et al.* (2007) 'What makes self-help interventions effective in the management of depressive symptoms? Meta-analysis and meta regression.' *Psychological Medicine 37*, 9, 1217–1228.

Girl Guides Association (2014) 'Girls' Attitudes Survey 2014.' Available at: www.girlguiding.org.uk/globalassets/docs-and-resources/research-and-campaigns/girls-attitudes-survey-2014.pdf, accessed on 19 February 2018.

Girl Guides Association (2015) 'Girls' Attitudes Survey 2015.' Available at: www.girlguiding.org.uk/globalassets/docs-and-resources/research-and-campaigns/girls-attitudes-survey-2015.pdf, accessed on 19 February 2018.

Girl Guides Association (2016) 'Girls' Attitudes Survey 2016.' Available at: https://www.girlguiding.org.uk/globalassets/docs-and-resources/research-and-campaigns/girls-attitudes-survey-2016.pdf, accessed on 19 February 2018.

Goodyer, I.M., Herbert, J. and Tamplin, A. (2003) 'Psychoendocrine antecedents of persistent first-episode major depression in adolescents: A community-based longitudinal enquiry.' *Psychological Medicine 33*, 601–610.

Greco, L.A. (2002) 'Creating a context of acceptance in child clinical and paediatric settings.' Paper presented at the annual meeting of the Association for the Advancement of Behavior Therapy, Reno, NV.

Greco, L.A. and Blomquist, K.K. (2006) 'Body Image, Eating Behaviour, and Quality of Life among Adolescent Girls: Role of Anxiety and Acceptance Processes in a School Sample.' In K.S. Berlin and A.R. Murrell (co-chairs) *Extending Acceptance and Mindfulness Research to Parents, Families and Adolescents: Process, Empirical Findings, Clinical Implications and Future Directions.* Symposium conducted at the Association for Behavior and Cognitive Therapies, Chicago, IL.

Greco, L.A., Blackledge, J.T., Coyne, L.W. and Ehrenreich, J. (2005) 'Integrating Acceptance and Mindfulness into Treatments for Child and Adolescent Anxiety Disorders: Acceptance and Commitment Therapy as an Example.' In S.M. Orsillo and L. Roemer (eds) *Acceptance and Mindfulness-Based Approaches to Anxiety: Conceptualization and Treatment.* New York: Springer Science.

Greco, L.A., Blomquist, K.K., Acra, S. and Moulton, D. (under review) 'Acceptance and commitment therapy for adolescents with functional abdominal pain: Results of a pilot investigation.' Manuscript submitted for publication. As cited in L.A. Greco and S.C. Hayes (2008) *Acceptance and Mindfulness Treatments for Children and Adolescents: A Practitioner's Guide.* Oakland, CA: New Harbinger Publications.

Green, H., McGinnity, A., Meltzer, H., Ford, T. and Goodman, R. (2005) *Mental Health of Children and Young People in Great Britain 2004*. London: Office for National Statistics Publication, Palgrave Macmillan.

Guasp, A. (2012) 'The school report. The experiences of gay young people in Britain's schools in 2012.' Available at: www.stonewall.org.uk/system/files/The_School_Report__2012_.pdf, accessed on 19 February 2018.

Harrington, R.C. and Dubicka, B. (2001) 'Natural History of Mood Disorders in Children and Adolescents.' In I. Goodyer (ed.) *The Depressed Child and Adolescent.* Cambridge: Cambridge University Press.

Hawton, K., Saunders, K.E. and O'Connor, R.C. (2012) 'Self-harm and suicide in adolescents.' *Lancet 379*, 2373–2382.

Hayes, L., Boyd, C.P. and Sewell, J. (2011) 'Acceptance and commitment therapy for the treatment of adolescent depression: A pilot study in a psychiatric outpatient setting.' *Mindfulness 2*, 2, 86–94.

Heffner, M., Sperry, J. and Eifert, G.H. (2002) 'Acceptance and commitment therapy in the treatment of an adolescent female with anorexia nervosa: A case example.' *Cognitive and Behavioural Practice* 9, 3, 232–236.

Hofman, S.G., Sawyer, A.T., Witt, A.A. and Oh, D. (2010) 'The effectiveness of mindfulness-based cognitive therapy on anxiety and depression: A meta-analytic review.' *Journal of Consulting and Clinical Psychology 78*, 2, 169–183.

Hollon, S., DeRubeis, R.J., Shelton, R.C., Amsterdam, J.D. *et al.* (2005) 'Prevention of relapse following cognitive therapy vs. medication in moderate to severe depression.' *Archives of General Psychiatry* 62, 417–422.

House of Commons Health Committee (2014) *Children's and Adolescents' Mental Health and CAMHS: Third Report of Session 2014–15, HC 342, London: The Stationary Office.* Available at: https://publications.parliament.uk/pa/cm201415/cmselect/cmhealth/342/342.pdf, accessed on 27 March 2018.

Huppert, F.A. and Johnson, D.M. (2010) 'A controlled trial of mindfulness-based training schools: The importance of practice for an impact on wellbeing.' *The Journal of Positive Psychology* 5, 4, 264–274.

Jacob, M.L., Keeley, M., Ritschel, L. and Craighead, W.E. (2013) 'Behavioural activation for the treatment of low-income, African American adolescents with major depressive disorder: A case series.' *Clinical Psychology and Psychotherapy 20*, 1, 87–96.

Jacobson, N.S., Martell, C.R. and Dimidjin, S. (2001) 'Behavioral activation treatment for depression: Returning to contextual roots.' *Clinical Psychology: Science and Practice* 8, 3, 255–270.

Jaffee, S.R., Moffitt, T.E., Caspi, A., Fombonne, E., Poulton, R. and Martin, J. (2002) 'Differences in early childhood risk factors for juvenile-onset and adult-onset depression.' *Archive of General Psychiatry 59*, 3, 215–222.

James, A.A.C.J., Soler, A. and Weatherall, R.R.W. (2005) 'Cognitive behavioural therapy for anxiety disorders in children and adolescents.' *Cochrane Database of Systematic Reviews 2005*, 4, CD004690.

Joyce, A., Etty-Leal, J., Zazryn, T., Hamilton, A. and Hassed, C. (2010) 'Exploring a mindfulness-based meditation program on the mental health of upper primary children: A pilot study.' *Advances in School Mental Health Promotion 3*, 17.

Kazdin, A.E. and Weisz, J.R. (1998) 'Identifying and developing empirically supported child and adolescent treatments.' *Journal of Consulting and Clinical Psychology 66*, 19–36.

Kendall, P.C., Flannery-Schroeder, E., Panichelli-Mindel, S.M., Sotham-Gerow, M., Henin, A. and Warman, M. (1997) 'Therapy with youths with anxiety disorders: A second randomized clinical trial.' *Journal of Consulting and Clinical Psychology 18*, 255–270.

Kendall, P.C., Safford, S., Flannery-Schroeder, E. and Webb, A. (2004) 'Child anxiety treatment: Outcomes in adolescence and impact on substance abuse and depression at 7.4 year follow-up.' *Journal of Consulting and Clinical Psychology 72*, 276–287.

Kennard, B.D., Emslie, G.J., Mayes, T.L., Nakonezny, P.A. *et al.* (2014) 'Sequential treatment with Fluoxetine and relapse-prevention CBT to improve outcomes in pediatric depression.' *American Journal of Psychiatry 171*, 10, 1083–1090.

Kessler, R.C., Berglund, P., Demler, O., Jin, R., Merikangas, K.R. and Walters, E.E. (2005) 'Lifetime prevalence and age-of-onset distributions of DSM-IV Disorders in the National Comorbidity Survey Replication.' *Archives of General Psychiatry 62*, 6, 593–602.

Kim-Cohen, J., Caspi, A., Moffitt, T.T., Harrington, H.I., Milne, B.J. and Poulton, R. (2003) 'Prior juvenile diagnoses in adults with mental disorder: Developmental follow-back of a prospective cohort.' *Archives of General Psychiatry 60*, 7, 709–717. Available at: www.ncbi.nlm.nih.gov/pubmed/12860775, accessed on 27 March 2018.

King, N.J., Molloy, G.N., Heyme, D., Murphy, G.C. and Ollendick, T. (1998) 'Emotive imagery treatment for childhood phobias: A credible and empirically validated intervention?' *Behavioural and Cognitive Psychotherapy 26*, 103–113.

Klein, J., Jacobs, R. and Reinecke, M. (2007) 'Cognitive-behavioural therapy for adolescent depression: A meta-analytic investigation of changes in effect-size estimates.' *Journal of the American Academy of Child and Adolescent Psychiatry 46*, 11, 1403–1413.

Kolko, D.J., Brent, D.A., Baugher, M., Bridge, J. and Birmaher, B. (2000) 'Cognitive and family therapies for adolescent depression: Treatment specificity, mediation and moderation.' *Journal of Consulting and Clinical Psychology* 68, 4, 603–614.

Korkodilos, M. (2016) *Reducing Child Mortality in London.* London: Public Health England. Available at: www.gov.uk/government/uploads/system/uploads/attachment_data/file/551123/Reducing_child_deaths_in_London.pdf, accessed on 18 February 2018.

Kovaacs, M. (1982) *The Children's Depression Inventory*. New York: Mental Health Systems.

Kuyken, W., Byford, S., Taylor, R.S., Watkins, E. *et al.* (2008) 'Mindfulness-based cognitive therapy to prevent relapse in recurrent depression.' *Journal of Consulting and Clinical Psychology 76*, 966–978.

Kuyken, W., Weare, K., Ukoumunne, O.C., Vicary, R. *et al.* (2013) 'Effectiveness of the Mindfulness in Schools Programme: Non-randomised controlled feasibility study.' *British Journal of Psychiatry 203*, 2, 126–131.

Lereya, S.T., Winsper, C., Heron, J., Lewis, G. *et al.* (2013) 'Being bullied during childhood and the prospective pathways to self-harm in late adolescence.' *Journal of the American Academy of Child and Adolescent Psychiatry 52*, 6, 608–618. Available at: www.ncbi.nlm.nih.gov/pubmed/23702450, accessed on 27 March 2018.

Lessof, C., Ross, A., Brind, R., Bell, E. and Newton, S. (2016) 'Longitudinal study of young people in England cohort 2: Health and wellbeing at wave 2. Research report.' Available at: www.gov.uk/government/uploads/system/uploads/attachment_data/file/599871/LSYPE2_w2-research_report.pdf, accessed on 19 February 2018.

Lin, L. yi., Sidani, J. E., Shensa, A., Radovic, A. *et al.* (2016) 'Association between social media use and depression among U.S. young adults.' *Depression and Anxiety 33*, 323–331.

Loeb, K.L., Wilson, G.T., Gilbert, J.S. and Labouvie, E. (2000) 'Guided and unguided self-help for binge eating.' *Behaviour Research and Therapy 38*, 3, 259–272.

Martin, S.D., Martin, E., Rai, S.S., Richardson, M.A. and Royall, R. (2001) 'Brain blood flow changes in depressed patients treated with interpersonal psychotherapy or Venlafaxine hydrochloride: Preliminary findings.' *Archives of General Psychiatry 58*, 7, 641–648.

McCauley, E., Schloredt, K.A., Gudmundsen, G., Martell, C. and Dimidjian, S. (2016) 'The Adolescent Behavioral Activation Program: Adapting behavioral activation as a treatment for depression in adolescence.' *Journal of Clinical Child and Adolescent Psychology 45*, 3, 291–304.

McManus, S., Meltzer, S., Brugha, T., Bebbington, P. and Jenkins, R. (2009) *Adult Psychiatric Morbidity in England, 2007: Results of a Household Survey.* Leeds: The Health and Social Care Information Centre.

Mental Health Foundation (2004) 'Lifetime impacts: Childhood and adolescent mental health – understanding the lifetime impacts.' Available at: www.mentalhealth.org.uk/sites/default/files/lifetime_impacts.pdf, accessed on 19 February 2018.

Mental Health Foundation (2006) *Truth Hurts: Report of the National Inquiry into Self-Harm Among Young People.* London: Mental Health Foundation.

Merikangas, K.R., He, J.P., Burstein, M., Swanson, S.A. *et al.* (2010) 'Lifetime prevalence of mental disorders in U.S. adolescents: Results from the National Comorbidity Survey Replication-Adolescent Supplement (NCS-A).' *Journal of the American Academy of Child and Adolescent Psychiatry 49*, 10, 980–989.

METRO (2014) 'Youth chances summary of first findings: The experiences of LGBTQ young people in England.' Available at: www.mermaidsuk.org.uk/assets/media/youth%20chances%20experiencies%20og%20lgbt%20youth_2014.pdf, accessed on 27 March 2018.

Mission Australia (2018) 'Youth Survey 2018.' Available at: www.missionaustralia.com.au/publications/youth-survey/823-mission-australia-youth-survey-report-2018/file, accessed on 20 February 2019.

Mojtabai, R., Olfson, M. and Han, B. (2016) 'National trends in the prevalence and treatment of depression in adolescents and young adults.' *Pediatrics 138*, 6. Available at: http://pediatrics.aappublications.org/content/pediatrics/138/6/e20161878.full.pdf, accessed on 19 February 2018.

MQ (2016) 'The MQ Manifesto for Young People's Mental Health.' Available at: www.mqmentalhealth.org/articles/mq-manifesto-for-young-peoples-mental-health, accessed on 27 March 2018.

Mufson, L., Dorta, K.P., Moreau, D. and Weissman, M.M. (2011) *Interpersonal Psychotherapy for Depressed Adolescents* (2nd edition). New York: Guilford Press.

Mufson, L., Dorta, K.P., Wickramaratne, P., Nomura, Y., Olfson, M. and Weissman, M.M. (2004) 'A randomised effectiveness trial of interpersonal psychotherapy for depressed adolescents.' *Archive of General Psychiatry 61*, 6, 577–584.

Murrell, A.R. and Scherbarth, A.J. (2006) 'State of the research and literature address: ACT with children, adolescents and parents.' *International Journal of Behavioral Consultation and Therapy 2*, 4, 531–543.

Naicker, K., Galambos, N.L., Zeng, Y., Senthilselvan, A. and Colman, I. (2013) 'Social demographic and health outcomes in the 10 years following adolescent depression.' *Journal of Adolescent Health 52*, 5, 533–538.

Napoli, M., Krech, P.R. and Holley, L.C. (2005) 'Mindfulness training for elementary school students: The Attention Academy.' *Journal of Applied School Psychology 21*, 99–125.

Nguyen, T., Hellebuyck, M., Halpern, M. and Fritze, D. (2018) 'The state of mental health in America.' Available at: www.mentalhealthamerica.net/sites/default/files/2018%20The%20State%20of%20MH%20in%20America%20-%20FINAL.pdf, accessed on 12 November 2018.

NICE (2005) *Depression in Children and Young People: Identification and Management.* London: NICE. Available at: www.nice.org.uk/guidance/cg28, accessed on 20 February 2019.

NICE (2009) *Depression in Adults: Recognition and Management.* London: NICE. Available at: www.nice.org.uk/guidance/cg90, accessed on 20 February 2019.

NICE (2010) *Promoting the Quality of Life of Looked After Children and Young People.* London: NICE. Available at: www.nice.org.uk/guidance/ph28, accessed on 27 March 2018.

Nodin, N., Peel, E., Tyler, A. and Rivers, I. (2014) 'The RaRE research report: LGB+T mental health – Risk and Resilience Explored.' Available at: www.queerfutures.co.uk/wp-content/uploads/2015/04/RARE_Research_Report_PACE_2015.pdf, accessed on 20 February 2018.

NSPCC (2014a) *Under Pressure. ChildLine Review: What's Affected Children in April 2013–March 2014.* London: NSPCC.

NSPCC (2014b) *On the Edge. ChildLine Spotlight: Suicide*. London: NSPCC. Available at: www.nspcc.org.uk/globalassets/documents/research-reports/on-the-edge-childline-suicide-report.pdf, accessed on 18 February 2018.

NSPCC (2016) *It Turned Out Someone Did Care. ChildLine Annual Review: 2015–16.* London: NSPCC.

NSPCC (2017) *Not Alone Anymore. ChildLine Annual Review: 2016–17*. London: NSPCC.

Nuffield Foundation (2013) *Social Trends and Mental Health: Introducing the Main Findings.* London: Nuffield Foundation.

Office for National Statistics (1997) *Psychiatric Morbidity among Young Offenders in England and Wales.* London: Office for National Statistics.

Office for National Statistics (2016) *Selected Children's Well-being Measures by Country* as quoted in Young Minds (2016) Young Minds Annual Report 2015-16. Available at: https://youngminds.org.uk/media/1233/youngminds-annual-report-15-16-final.pdf, accessed on 27 March 2018.

Office for National Statistics (2017) *Young People's Well-Being: 2017.* London: Office for National Statistics. Available at: www.ons.gov.uk/peoplepopulationandcommunity/wellbeing/articles/youngpeopleswellbeingandpersonalfinance/2017, accessed on 19 February 2018.

O'Kearney, R.T., Anstey, K., von Sanden, C. and Hunt, A. (2006) 'Behavioural and cognitive behavioural therapy for obsessive compulsive disorder in children and adolescents.' *Cochrane Database of Systematic Reviews 2006*, 4, CD004856.

Patalay, P. and Fitzsimons, E. (2017) *Mental Ill-Health among Children of the New Century: Trends Across Childhood with a Focus on Age 14.* London: Centre for Longitudinal Studies. Available at: www.ncb.org.uk/sites/default/files/uploads/documents/Research_reports/UCL%20-%20NCB%20-%20Mental_Ill-Health%20FINAL.pdf, accessed on 19 February 2018.

Pavlov, I.P. (1927) *Conditioned Reflexes: An Investigation of the Physiological Activity of the Cerebral Cortex.* Translated and edited by G.V. Anrep. London: Oxford University Press.

Perou, R., Bitsko, R.H., Blumberg, S.J., Pastor, P. *et al.* (2013) 'Mental health surveillance among children: United States, 2005–2011.' *MMWR Surveillance Summary 62*, 2, 1–35.

Piet, J. and Hougaard, E. (2011) 'The effect of mindfulness-based cognitive therapy for prevention of relapse in recurrent major depression: A systematic review and meta-analysis.' *Clinical Psychology Review 31*, 6, 1032–1040.

Pryzbylski, A., Murayama, K., DeHaan, C. and Gladwell, V. (2013) 'Motivational, emotional and behavioural correlates of fear of missing out.' *Computers in Human Behaviour 29*, 4, 1841–1848.

Public Health England (2016) 'The mental health of children and young people in England.' Available at: www.cumbria.gov.uk/eLibrary/Content/Internet/537/6381/4278314423.pdf, accessed on 19 February 2018.

Rapee, R.M., Wignall, A., Hudson, J.L. and Schniering, C.A. (2000) *Treating Anxious Children and Adolescents: An Evidence-Based Approach.* Oakland, CA: New Harbinger Publications.

Rees, G. and Main, G. (eds) (2015) *Children's Views on Their Lives and Well-Being in 15 Countries: An Initial Report on the Children's Worlds Survey, 2013/14.* York: Children's Worlds Project (ISCWeB). Available at: www.isciweb.org/_Uploads/dbsAttachedFiles/ChildrensWorlds2015-FullReport-Final.pdf, accessed on 27 March 2018.

Ritschel, L.A., Ramirez, C.L., Jones, M. and Craighead, W.E. (2011) 'Behavioural activation for depressed teens: A pilot study.' *Cognitive and Behavioral Practice 18*, 2, 281–299.

Rosen, R. (2016) '"The perfect generation": Is the internet undermining young people's mental health?' Available at: https://parentzone.org.uk/system/files/attachments/The%20Perfect%20Generation%20report.pdf, accessed on 19 February 2018.

Royal Society for Public Health (2017) '#StatusOfMind: Social media and young people's mental health and wellbeing.' Available at: www.rsph.org.uk/uploads/assets/uploaded/62be270a-a55f-4719-ad668c2ec7a74c2a.pdf, accessed on 19 February 2018.

Rush, A.J., Kraemer, H.C., Sackeim, H.S., Fava, M. *et al.* (2006) 'Report by the ACNP task force on response and remission in major depressive disorder.' *Neuropsychopharmacology 31*, 9, 1841–1853.

Rush, A.J., Trivedi, M.H., Ibrahim, H.M., Carmody, T.J. *et al.* (2003) 'The 16-item Quick Inventory of Depressive Symptomatology (QIDS), clinician rating (QIDS-C), and self-report (QIDS-SR): A psychometric evaluation in patients with chronic major depression.' *Biological Psychiatry 54*, 5, 573–583.

Sadler, K., Vizard, T., Ford, T., Marcheselli, F. *et al.* (2018) *Mental Health of Children and Young People in England 2017: Summary of Key Findings*, London: NHS Digital.

Sampasa-Kanyinga, H. and Lewis, R.F. (2015) 'Frequent use of social networking sites is associated with poor psychological functioning among children and adolescents.' *Cyberpsychology, Behavior, and Social Networking 18*, 7, 380–385.

Schonert-Reichl, K.A. and Lawlor, M.S. (2010) 'The effects of a mindfulness-based education program on pre- and early adolescents' well-being and social and emotional competence.' *Mindfulness 1*, 137–151.

Scogin, F., Bynum, J., Stephens, G. and Calhoon, S. (1990) 'Efficacy of self-administered treatment programs: Meta-analytic review.' *Professional Psychology: Research and Practice 21*, 1, 42–47.

Segal, Z.V., Bieling, P., Young, T., MacQueen, G. *et al.* (2010) 'Antidepressant monotherapy vs sequential pharmacotherapy and mindfulness-based cognitive therapy, or placebo, for relapse prophylaxis in recurrent depression.' *Archives of General Psychiatry 67*, 1256–1264.

Seligman, M.E.P. (1995) 'The effectiveness of psychotherapy: The Consumer Reports Study.' *American Psychologist 50*, 12, 965–974.

Sempik, J. and Becker, S. (2013) 'Young adult carers at school: Experiences and perceptions of caring and education.' Available at: https://professionals.carers.org/sites/default/files/media/young_adult_carers_at_school_-_summary.pdf, accessed on 25 February 2019.

Sempik, J., Ward, H. and Darker, I. (2008) 'Emotional and behavioural difficulties of children and young people at entry into care.' *Clinical Child Psychology and Psychiatry 13*, 2, 221–233.

Semple, R. and Lee, J. (2011) *Mindfulness-Based Cognitive Therapy for Anxious Children*. Oakland, CA: New Harbinger.

Silverman, W.K., Kurtines, W.M., Ginsburg, G.S., Weems, C.F., Rabian, B. and Setafini, L.T. (1999) 'Contingency management, self-control and education support in the treatment of childhood phobic disorders: A randomized clinical trial.' *Journal of Consulting and Clinical Psychology 67*, 675–687.

Skinner, B.F. (1938) *The Behavior of Organisms*. New York: Appleton-Century-Crofts.

Smith, P., Yule, W., Perrin, S., Tranah, T., Dalgleish, T. and Clark, D.M. (2007) 'Cognitive-behavioral therapy for PTSD in children and adolescents: A preliminary randomized controlled trial.' *Journal of the American Academy of Child and Adolescent Psychiatry 46*, 8, 1051–1061.

Spence, S., Donovan, C. and Brechman-Toussaint, M. (2000) 'The treatment of childhood social phobia: The effectiveness of a social skills training-based cognitive behavioural intervention with and without parental involvement.' *Journal of Child Psychology and Psychiatry 41*, 713–726.

Strauss, P., Cook, A., Winter, S., Watson, V., Wright Toussaint, D., Lin, A. (2017). *Trans Pathways: the mental health experiences and care pathways of trans young people. Summary of results. Telethon Kids Institute, Perth, Australia.* Available at: https://www.telethonkids.org.au/globalassets/media/documents/brain--behaviour/trans-pathwayreport-web2.pdf, accessed on 20 April 2019.

Teasdale, J.D., Segal, Z.V., Williams, M.G., Ridgeway, V.A., Soulsby, J.M. and Lau, M.A. (2000) 'Prevention of relapse/recurrence in major depression by mindfulness-based cognitive therapy.' *Journal of Consulting and Clinical Psychology 68*, 4, 615–623.

Thapar, A., Collishaw, S., Potter, R. and Thapar, A. (2010) 'Managing and preventing depression in adolescents.' *British Medical Journal 340*, 7740, 254–258.

Tindall, L., Mikocka-Walus, A., McMillan, D., Wright, B., Hewitt, C. and Gascoyne, S. (2017) 'Is behavioural activation effective in the treatment of depression in young people? A systematic review and meta-analysis.' *Psychology and Psychotherapy: Theory, Research and Practice 90*, 4, 770–796.

Treatment for Adolescents with Depression Study (2004) 'Fluoxetine, cognitive behavioral therapy and their combination for adolescents with depression: Treatment for Adolescents with Depression Study (TADS) randomized controlled trial.' *Journal of the American Medical Association 292*, 807–820.

Treatment for Adolescents with Depression Study (2007) 'The Treatment for Adolescents with Depression Study (TADS): Long term effectiveness and safety outcomes.' *Archives of General Psychiatry 64*, 1132–1144.

van Aalderen, J., Donders, A., Giommi, F., Spinhoven, P., Barendregt, H. and Speckens, A. (2011) 'The efficacy of mindfulness-based cognitive therapy in recurrent depressed patients with and without a current depressive episode: A randomized controlled trial.' *Psychological Medicine 3*, 1–13.

Vickery, C.E. and Dorjee, D. (2016) 'Mindfulness training in primary schools decreases negative affect and increases meta-cognition in children.' *Frontiers in Psychology 6*, 2025.

Walter, G. and Ghaziuddin, N. (2009) 'Using Other Biologic Treatments: Electro-Convulsive Therapy, Transcranial Magnetic Stimulation, Vagus Nerve Stimulation and Light Therapy.' In J.M. Rey and B. Birmaher (eds) *Treating Child and Adolescent Depression*. Philadelphia, PA: Wolters Kluwer, Lippincott Williams & Wilkins.

Watanabe, N., Hunot, V., Omori, I.M., Churchill, R. and Furukawa, T.A. (2007) 'Psychotherapy for depression among children and adolescents: A systematic review.' *Acta Psychiatrica Scandinavica 116*, 2, 84–95.

Weisz, J.R. and Kazdin, A.E. (2010) *Evidence Based Psychotherapies for Children and Adolescents*. New York: Guilford Press.

Weisz, J.R., McCarty, C.A. and Valeri, S.M. (2006) 'Effects of psychotherapy for depression in children and aolescents: A meta-analysis.' *Psychology Bulletin 132*, 132–149.

Williams, C., Wilson, P., Morrison, J., McMahon, A. *et al.* (2013) 'Guided self-help cognitive behavioural therapy for depression in primary care: A randomised controlled trial.' *PLoS ONE 8*, 1, e52735, Available at: https://journals.plos.org/plosone/article?id=10.1371/journal.pone.0052735, accessed on 19 February 2018.

Williams, M. and Penman, D. (2011) *Mindfulness: A Practical Guide to Finding Peace in a Frantic World.* London: Piatkus.

Wolfe, I., Macfarlane, A., Donkin, A., Marmot, M. and Viner, R. (2014) 'Why children die: Death in infants, children and young people in the UK. Part A: May 2014.' Royal College of Paediatrics and Child Health, National Children's Bureau and British Association for Child and Adolescent Public Health. Available at: www.ncb.org.uk/sites/default/files/uploads/documents/Policy_docs/why_children_die_full_report.pdf, accessed on 25 February 2019.

World Health Organization (2001) 'The World Health Report 2001. Mental health: New understanding, new hope.' Available at: www.who.int/whr/2001/en/whr01_en.pdf?ua=1, accessed on 20 February 2019.

World Health Organization (2003) 'Caring for children and adolescents with mental disorders: Setting WHO directions.' Available at: www.who.int/mental_health/media/en/785.pdf, accessed on 14 March 2018.

World Health Organzation (2014) 'Adolescents: Health risks and solutions.' Available at: www.who.int/mediacentre/factsheets/fs345/en, accessed on 30 October 2018.

World Health Organization (2017) 'Depression and other common mental health disorders: Global estimates.' Available at: www.who.int/mental_health/management/depression/prevalence_global_health_estimates/en, accessed on 19 February 2018.

YouGov (2016) 'One in four students suffer from mental health problems.' Available at: https://yougov.co.uk/topics/lifestyle/articles-reports/2016/08/09/quarter-britains-students-are-afflicted-mental-hea, accessed on 19 February 2018.

YouGov/MQ and Forster (2016) 'Mental illness research: children, April 2016' as quoted in MQ (2016) *The MQ Manifesto for Young People's Mental Health.* Available at: https://www.mqmentalhealth.org/articles/mq-manifesto-for-young-peoples-mental-health, accessed on 19 April 2019.

Young, J.F., Mufson, L. and Davies, M. (2006) 'Efficacy of interpersonal psychotherapy–adolescent skills training: An indicated preventive intervention for depression.' *Journal of Child Psychology and Psychiatry 47*, 12, 1254–1262.

YoungMinds (2011) 'Depression and your child: Your guide to the signs and helping them find support.' Available at: https://youngminds.org.uk/media/1515/young-minds-depression-your-child.pdf, accessed on 19 February 2018.

YoungMinds (2016) 'YoungMinds Annual Report 2015–16.' Available at: https://youngminds.org.uk/media/1233/youngminds-annual-report-15-16-final.pdf, accessed on 27 March 2018.

Zhou, X., Hetrick, S.E., Cuijpers, P., Qin, B. *et al.* (2015) 'Comparative efficacy and acceptability of psychotherapies for depression in children and adolescents: A systematic review and network meta-analysis.' *World Psychiatry 14*, 2, 207–222.